WE DEMAND DECENT HOUSING NOW!
WE DEMAND EQUAL RIGHTS NOW!
WE MARCH TOGETHER CATHOLIC JEWS PROTESTANT FOR DIGNITY AND BROTHERHOOD OF ALL MEN UNDER GOD NOW!
WE MARCH FOR EFFECTIVE CIVIL RIGHTS
WE MARCH FOR INTEGRATED SCHOOLS
WE DEMAND EQUAL RIGHTS NOW!
WE MARCH FOR INTEGRATED SCHOOLS
WE DEMAND AN END TO BIAS NOW!

"In *Troublemaker for Justice* children and teens can finally discover the story of the man who possibly was the most influential person in the struggle for Civil Rights—Bayard Rustin. They'll discover a man who was behind many, if not most, Civil Rights and human rights efforts in the United States and around the world in the 1940s-1980s. They'll discover a man who was willing to work behind the scenes, who was willing to be in the background in photos, and who was willing to work for a purpose, not for praise or notoriety. They'll discover an African American gay man who never forgot his Quaker roots and who sought to peacefully create social justice so that equality became more than a word, it became a reality. This carefully researched book is one that children, teenagers, and adults should read and discuss, and the life of Bayard Rustin is one we should all emulate."—**Rob Sanders**, author of *Pride: The Story of Harvey Milk and the Rainbow Flag*

"Written with verve and an unerring eye for the important details, as well as the larger picture, *Troublemaker for Justice* is a nuanced, vital, and compelling portrait of civil rights leader Bayard Rustin. It is beautifully imagined and positioned perfectly in a thrilling sweep of U.S. history. Rustin's life was a series of breakneck collisions with history and *Troublemaker for Justice* captures the energy and importance of his personal and political life. Perfect for any reader young adult or older, who wants to know more about Rustin, social justice movements, and how brave, visionary people have changed American history and made all of our lives better."—**Michael Bronski**, author of *A Queer History of the United States*

"*Troublemaker for Justice* will thrill and inspire young readers—and their parents. Bayard Rustin was a crucial figure in the Civil Rights movement, and everyone should know his story, but even more importantly, we need his principles and his tactics now more than ever. This is one history book that could help you change the future." —**Charlie Jane Anders**, author of *The City in the Middle of the Night*

"*Troublemaker for Justice* is an incredible book! It is hard to believe that so much tumultuous history is contained in 154 pages. What emerges is the intense importance of seeing Bayard and other Civil

Rights Leaders not just as historical figures, but as the brave people they were who made sacrifices for the betterment of society. Their stories vehemently ask us to not let their work towards creating a less violent world be in vain."—**Connie Griffin**, Children's Book Specialist, Bookworks, Albuquerque, NM

"Packed full of sidebars with additional context—including regarding the Quakers' views of civil rights, the nonviolent philosophy of Mahatma Gandhi, and Jim Crow laws—the book also lists additional resources, includes a timeline of Rustin's life, and forwards discussion questions. . . . *Troublemaker for Justice* is a helpful primer for young readers about a civil rights leader who's worth learning more about."— *Foreword Magazine*

"In today's political landscape, this volume is a lesson in the courage to live according to one's truth and the dedication it takes to create a better world. An essential guide to the life of Bayard Rustin, architect of critical movements for freedom and justice." — *Kirkus* (starred review)

"Though little remembered today, Bayard Rustin was a major leader of the American civil rights movement, a mentor of Dr. Martin Luther King Jr., and a chief organizer of the historic 1963 March on Washington for Jobs and Freedom. A committed pacifist and believer in the power of nonviolence, Rustin was actively involved in civil rights protests, landing himself in prison 20 times by 1969. His commitment to human rights found expression not only in the U.S. but internationally as well. So why is he largely unsung? The authors argue it is because he was openly gay. While presenting a posthumous Presidential Medal of Freedom to Rustin, President Barack Obama confirmed this, saying, "This great leader . . . was denied his rightful place in history because he was openly gay." The three authors of this thoughtful and informative biography—the narrative text of which is greatly amplified by a generous collection of black-and-white pictures and sidebar features—have gone a long way to rectifying this injustice. . . . This biography is an indispensable addition to the literature of both civil and gay rights." — *Booklist* (starred review)

TROUBLE MAKER FOR JUSTICE

THE STORY OF BAYARD RUSTIN, THE MAN BEHIND THE MARCH ON WASHINGTON

Jacqueline Houtman
Walter Naegle
Michael G. Long

City Lights Books | San Francisco

Troublemaker for Justice was first published in 2014 in a limited edition produced by Quaker Press of Friends General Conference as *Bayard Rustin: The Invisible Activist.*

Cover photo of Bayard Rustin courtesy of the Estate of Bayard Rustin
Cover design by Linda Ronan

Layout and composition by David Botwinick
Book design by Linda Ronan

ISBN: 9780872867659
e-ISBN: 9780872867987

Library of Congress Cataloging-in-Publication Data

Names: Houtman, Jacqueline, author. | Naegle, Walter, author. | Long,
    Michael G., author.
Title: Trouble maker for justice : the story of Bayard Rustin, the man
    behind the march on Washington / Jacqueline Houtman, Walter Naegl,
    Michael G. Long.
Description: San Francisco : City Lights Books, [2019] | Includes
    bibliographical references. | Audience: Age: 13. | Audience: Grade 7 to 8.
Identifiers: LCCN 2019018987 (print) | LCCN 2019021919 (ebook) | ISBN
    9780872867659
Subjects: LCSH: Rustin, Bayard, 1912-1987—Juvenile literature. | Civil
    rights workers—United States—Juvenile literature. | African American
    civil rights workers—Juvenile literature. | African Americans—Civil
    rights—History—20th century—Juvenile literature. | Civil rights
    movements—United States—History—20th century—Juvenile literature. |
    United States—Race relations—History—20th century—Juvenile
    literature.
Classification: LCC E185.97.R93 H688 2019 (print) | LCC E185.97.R93
    (ebook) | DDC 323.092 [B]—dc23
LC record available at https://lccn.loc.gov/2019018987
LC ebook record available at https://lccn.loc.gov/2019021919

City Lights Books are published at the City Lights Bookstore
261 Columbus Avenue, San Francisco, CA 94133
www.citylights.com

CONTENTS

PREFACE

"We need, in every community, a group of angelic troublemakers."

When Bayard Rustin spoke these words, he knew all too well that social problems—violence, poverty, and racial, religious, and ethnic divisions—often divide our human community.

More importantly, Bayard also believed that everyday people, including children and youth, can heal this brokenness. He was convinced beyond a shadow of a doubt that we—you and I—have the power to create a place where we can enjoy peace, unity, and economic justice.

To make the world better, according to Bayard, we have to be *troublemakers*—people who refuse to cooperate with anyone or anything that supports racism, sexism, poverty, and violence as a means for dealing with human conflict.

We have to say *No!* to those who use force. *No!* to those who demean people because of their ethnic origin, religion, sexual orientation, or the color of their skin. And *No!* to those who refuse to help poor people of any color.

We have to be *angelic*, too, as we raise our voices.

Even as we say *No!*, we must also say *Yes!* to nonviolence. *Yes!* to working cooperatively. And *Yes!* to freedom from poverty—and to equality for all.

This book is our attempt to introduce a new generation of young readers to Bayard Rustin's hope for a chorus of angelic troublemakers who can and will create a better world.

When we started this book, we really wanted to reach you, our young readers, partly because of our knowledge that young people are often the ones who have the fresh ideas and boundless energy required to turn the world upside down. When nations undergo dramatic transformation for the better, it's often because young people are leading the way. Because we know of your power to make the world better, we wanted this book to be in your hands.

We wanted you to read this book because we truly believe that the life of Bayard Rustin can inspire and educate you and other young angelic-troublemakers-in-the-making.

In reading about his life, you will encounter a leading expert in angelic troublemaking—a man who was courageous enough to go to jail for his belief in nonviolence during World War II, who was smart enough to organize the 1963 March on Washington for Jobs and Freedom, and who was humble enough to help young leaders like Martin Luther King, Jr. become important figures in the nonviolent struggle for civil and human rights.

If you let him, Bayard Rustin can inspire and teach you, too.

His words and actions can help you think about angelic ideas (like nonviolence, freedom, and equality). They can inspire you to stand up for your beliefs about these ideals. And they can assist you in developing creative strategies for troublemaking (methods like conversations and negotiations, sit-ins and rallies, marches, and boycotts).

Bayard has certainly inspired each of us—the three authors.

As a high school student in the 1960s, Walter Naegle was fascinated by the African American struggle for civil rights and the notion of resisting injustice nonviolently. Bayard was a leading movement strategist, and when they met years later, they fell in love.

Michael Long first learned about Bayard when reading a book about Martin Luther King, Jr. Michael was so impressed by Bayard's angelic troublemaking that he decided, with help from Walter, to edit a book of Bayard's letters—and to march against war several times since September 11, 2001.

Jacqueline Houtman learned a little about Bayard through her Quaker Meeting. She was thrilled when Walter, Michael, and QuakerPress asked her to help them make Bayard's life come alive for young readers. As she worked on the book, she listened to recordings of Bayard's voice. As she learned more about him, she became convinced that Bayard's story needed to be told widely to young (and not-so-young) audiences.

Walter, Michael, and Jacqueline collaborated on the manuscript, each contributing to the process with their own skills and insights. Together we produced a book that we believe is better than any of us could have written on our own.

Because of our own experiences with the magnetic quality of Bayard's life, we have a hunch that you too may join us someday in the chorus of angelic troublemakers.

Don't worry if your voice soars higher than ours ever did. In fact, we are hoping that you and others will carry on Bayard's non-violent life and legacy in ways we cannot even begin to imagine as we look toward the future that belongs to you.

So enjoy the pages ahead and then go make some trouble—angelically.

A FEW WORDS ABOUT WORDS

The words we use to describe ourselves and each other can be respectful, insulting, or hurtful. The meanings and emotional impact of those words change over time. Bayard lived in an earlier time, when the words and their meanings were different. He was exposed to some very hurtful language because of the color of his skin and his sexual orientation. We think it is important for readers to know about that. It is part of our shared history.

In choosing words for this book, we tried to be as respectful as possible, while still capturing the challenges faced by Bayard and others at that time. We use both "African American" and "black." In most cases, we use "white" to describe Americans of European descent. When we use the words "black" and "white," we generally use them as adjectives rather than nouns, since skin color is just one way to describe people, and should not define them. We use the words "gay," "lesbian," and "homosexual" to describe sexual orientation. Although "homosexual" is considered by some to be an outdated term, it was often the preferred term during Bayard's life.

Bayard knew the power of words. He knew words could affect people's emotions, beliefs, and lives.

The March on Washington for Jobs and Freedom, August 28, 1963. The crowd, estimated at 250,000, was the largest ever assembled in Washington, DC.

chapter 1

OUT OF THE SHADOWS

On a hot August afternoon in 1963, Bayard Rustin stood on the steps of the Lincoln Memorial in Washington, DC. In front of him, a sea of people stretched all the way to the Washington Monument and along the reflecting pool in between. Some had even climbed the trees that lined the sides of the reflecting pool to get a better view. Although most of the people in the crowd were African American like Bayard, people of all races stood together, some even holding hands. There was no *whites only* section in this crowd.

Reverend Martin Luther King, Jr. stood at the podium. "I have a dream that my four little children will one day live in a nation where they will not be judged by the color of their skin but by the content of their character."[1]

Then came Bayard's turn. He stepped out of the shadows to read the words he had prepared. This was Bayard's moment, but his name was not even printed on the official program of the March on Washington for Jobs and Freedom. Everyone knows about the "I Have a Dream" speech, but who knows what Bayard had to say that day?

Today, Martin Luther King, Jr. is a familiar name. Although he was only 39 years old when he was assassinated in 1968, King is remembered as one of the most important civil rights leaders in

Some folks cooled off by dangling their feet in the reflecting pool.

Bayard Rustin stood behind Dr. King during his speech.

United States history. We commemorate his birthday with a federal holiday. Hundreds of streets across the nation are named after him. A thirty-foot-tall granite statue of King stands near the site of the March.

But who remembers Bayard Rustin? Who remembers that he went to jail for opposing war? Who remembers that he helped to teach King the value of nonviolence? Who remembers that he was arrested for sitting in the *whites only* section of a bus thirteen years before Rosa Parks refused to give up her seat to a white man? Who remembers all the work he did fighting bigotry, segregation, militarism, and nuclear weapons? Who remembers that he organized the March on Washington for Jobs and Freedom, which up to that point had been the largest nonviolent demonstration for civil rights in US history?

Bayard Rustin was one of the most influential civil rights leaders, but very few people know his name.

Bayard's grandmother, Julia Davis Rustin, was the first black student at Friends' Graded School, a Quaker school now known as West Chester Friends School.

chapter 2

ONE BIG FAMILY

Bayard Taylor Rustin grew up in Julia and Janifer Rustin's "big old house" in West Chester, Pennsylvania, twenty-five miles from Philadelphia. Its ten rooms were filled with Rustin children, neighbors, and visiting strangers. It was "a hubbub," Bayard remembered. "People were coming and going" throughout the day. The dominant figure in the house, and in Bayard's early life, was Julia Davis Rustin, known to her neighbors as "Ma Rustin." Bayard later described her as a "dealer in relieving misery," devoted to helping people in need.[2] She worked tirelessly to improve the lives of those around her because she believed that every human being deserves respect and dignity. With Julia's guidance, Bayard grew up to do the same.

Quakers and Slavery

Quakers believe that the light of God is within everyone and everyone deserves to be respected and treated kindly. Near the end of the seventeenth century, some Quakers came to see that enslavement of human beings contradicted their belief in the equality of every person. Slavery was wrong. After the Revolutionary War, Quakers urged each other to free any enslaved people they owned. Some Quakers helped escaping African Americans, worked to abolish the institution of slavery, and educated freed men, women, and children.

Bayard's grandfather, Janifer Rustin, was born into slavery in Laplata, Maryland, in 1864. He was freed a year later, when the Thirteenth Amendment abolished slavery, and he moved to West Chester, Pennsylvania as a young man in the 1880s.

Bayard (center, second row, in a light jacket) sang in the choir at Bethel African Methodist Episcopal Church.

Julia was born in 1873 and spent her childhood in the home of Quaker Congressman, Thomas Butler, where her mother worked as a maid. The Butlers saw to it that Julia received a good education in a local Quaker school and later at nursing school. It was rare at this time for African American women to attend school with white students and train to become nurses. It was also rare for black and white people to attend the same church, but Julia Davis and her parents worshiped with white Quakers at the local Quaker meetinghouse.

Julia married Janifer Rustin in 1891. Although raised as a Quaker, she joined the Bethel African Methodist Episcopal (AME) Church when she married. Unlike the Quaker Meeting, the Bethel AME Church was an all-black community.

Julia and Janifer Rustin had six daughters and two sons. Bayard (rhymes with "fired") was born on March 17, 1912 and was probably named for Bayard Taylor, a local Quaker poet. For the first years of his life, Bayard believed that Julia and Janifer were his

What Do Quakers Believe?

Quakers seek to lead their lives as an outward expression of the belief that each person can have a direct experience of the Inner Light. To that end they practice:

- *Pacifism and nonviolence*: Opposition to war and violence is one of the best-known of the Quaker testimonies.
- *Equality*: No individual is more deserving of rights and respect than anyone else.
- *Integrity*: The truth is very important to Quakers and they strive to make their actions consistent with their values.
- *Simplicity*: Concern with outward appearance and possessions is a distraction from spiritual matters.

mother and father until one of his school classmates teased him, saying that Julia and Janifer were not his real parents. He ran home to Julia after school and she told him the truth. Her eldest daughter, Florence, whom Bayard thought of as his sister, was really his mother and his other "brothers" and "sisters" were really his uncles and aunts. Florence was nineteen and unmarried when Bayard was born. Bayard's father, Archie Hopkins, showed no interest in marrying Florence or being a parent to their newborn son. Julia and Janifer, Bayard's grandparents, decided to raise Bayard as their son. "Florence is your mother," said Julia, "but we're one big family and we are all mothers for everybody."[3] This was true in the Rustin family, and formed the basis for Bayard's lifetime belief in the unity of the human family.

Ma Rustin was the main moral influence in young Bayard's life. She passed on many of the values she had learned from her Quaker upbringing and she and Janifer made sure that Bayard spent a great deal of time at Bethel AME Church.

Julia's Quaker upbringing and her experiences at Bethel AME had convinced her that every person was a valuable member of the human family and had equal worth and dignity. She told Bayard that it was everyone's duty "to treat each person as a complete human being," not as an inferior, unworthy of respect.[4]

But Bayard did not always follow his grandmother's lesson.

When he was in fifth grade, he and a group of white boys threw rocks and chanted an offensive, racist verse at the Chinese American owner of a local laundry service. When Julia found out, she made Bayard work at the laundry after school for two weeks without pay. This was not merely punishment. It was an opportunity for Bayard to learn that people of all races belong to the human family. It also taught Bayard how peer pressure can cause people to do bad things they wouldn't do on their own. "I knew it was wrong to do, but I've never forgotten that little verse," he later recalled, "or my grandmother's reaction to how I could have done such a thing."[5]

Throughout his life, Bayard followed the Quaker tradition of pacifism and nonviolence, which he also learned from Julia. She insisted that her children should use only peaceful ways to resolve conflict. "We were taught that it was too tiresome to hate," Bayard recalled.[6]

Ma Rustin was a pacifist, but she was not passive. She was committed to nonviolence, but she would not stand silently by while others were being treated unfairly. She told Bayard that it was impor-

Quakers: The Religious Society of Friends

The Religious Society of Friends (Quakers) began in England in the seventeenth century. Early Quakers (also called Friends with a capital F) discovered that every person could experience God's spirit, the Inner Light, in themselves and others. They worshipped together in silence, without the assistance of an ordained priest. Recognizing that the Inner Light is in every person, Quakers came to believe in the equality of all people, and that killing and war were wrong.

Quakers were persecuted for their beliefs, and many left England for North America. A large group of them settled in the colony established by William Penn, a British Quaker, who founded Pennsylvania as a place where all could be free to worship as they wanted and Friends' principles could be tested. There was still a sizable population of Quakers in the Philadelphia area, including West Chester, when Bayard was growing up.

tant to stand up for equal rights and human dignity when he saw prejudice and discrimination. She would not strike or insult those who discriminated against her, but she would not cower or run

> You need not always weep
> and mourn,
>
> Let my people go!
>
> And wear these slav'ry chains
> forlorn,
>
> Let my people go!
>
> Go down, Moses,
>
> Way down in Egypt's land;
>
> Tell old Pharaoh
>
> To let my people go!
>
> — African American
>   Spiritual, Go Down Moses

away when confronted by injustice, especially racial prejudice. She was an early member of the National Association for the Advancement of Colored People (NAACP), an organization dedicated to using education and the legal system to help African Americans gain constitutional rights long denied them.

Always willing to help out in her community, Julia started a daycare center and summer Bible camp for African American children. She told the biblical story in which Moses liberated the Israelites in Egypt and led them to the Promised Land—a land of freedom, flowing with milk and honey so no one would go hungry.

Julia also welcomed strangers into her home, African Americans who were leaving the South looking for their own Promised Land. Many in the rural South were forced to do hard work for extremely low wages, and the area continued to be a dangerous place for them. With few possessions, they walked north to find greater freedom and jobs with a decent income in big cities like Philadelphia, Chicago, Detroit, and New York. People like Julia provided shelter and food for these weary folks along the way. Sometimes she woke Bayard up in the middle of the night and hustled him out of his bed so that a tired traveler could sleep there.

One night, Bayard was awakened by "the most extraordinary moaning and groaning" from the next room, where a traveling family slept. Then he smelled gas. He alerted his grandfather and they found the family "in very serious trouble."[7] Unfamiliar with the gas lighting used in cities in those days, they had put out the flame before going to sleep, as they had done with the oil lamps they knew. But they hadn't turned off the illuminating gas, which contained toxic fumes and filled the room. Everyone survived, but it was a traumatic experience for young Bayard.

The Rustins also opened their home to important African

American leaders like W.E.B. Du Bois, James Weldon Johnson, and Mary McLeod Bethune. When they visited the area, they could not stay in local hotels, reserved for *whites only*. As an active member of the NAACP, Julia invited them to sleep at the Rustin home, where Bayard often heard them talking about issues affecting their community, such as segregation and discrimination.

Bayard felt safe and valued in his home with Julia and Janifer. He knew bad things happened to black people because of discrimination, but he had not experienced them himself.

At least not yet.

Bayard in elementary school (middle row, second from left).

chapter 3

STEAL AWAY

Julia fought for equal rights for all, but she fought especially fiercely for Bayard. When his elementary school teachers tried to change her grandson from a left-handed writer to a right-handed one, as was the custom at the time, Julia marched into the principal's office. She demanded that they allow Bayard—a natural leftie—to write with his left hand. Once he was allowed to follow his natural tendencies instead of trying to be what he wasn't, Bayard was free to focus his time and energies on schoolwork. And he excelled.

One of Bayard's most influential teachers was Helena Robinson. She taught her sixth grade students about the evils of slavery, about how people who came to America from Europe (and their descendants) took people from Africa to America and forced them to work. She taught her students about racial discrimination and oppression. It was from Robinson that Bayard became aware of the cruelty of lynching. She explained that mobs of white Southerners would attack and publicly murder African Americans to assert their power through intimidation and fear. Bayard had no real experience with this kind of brutality, at least not as a young child. "Nobody in my neighborhood ever got lynched," he later recalled. "It was about blacks being beaten because they talked to a white woman, but nobody in my neighborhood could not talk to a white woman."[8]

LC-USZ62-7816

Harriet Tubman (1823 – 1913)
nurse, spy and scout

Harriet Tubman, who had escaped from slavery in Maryland, was one of the most famous conductors of the Underground Railroad. Tubman traveled to the South nineteen times to escort more than 300 African Americans to a new life in the North. Known as "Moses," she sometimes sang a spiritual, "Steal Away to Jesus," as a secret way to let enslaved men, women, and children know she was planning an escape during her visit with them.

14

The Underground Railroad

The Underground Railroad began in the early nineteenth century. Abolitionists, including many Quakers, came up with a system to help people escape from owners who broke up their families, beat them with whips, and denied them a basic education.

Abolitionists used the language of railroad life to describe their roles and actions in helping African Americans escape from the South. "Conductors," for example, escorted and guided them on the passage to freedom, secretly moving them from place to place. Some members of the Rustin family's church, Bethel AME, served as conductors during the nineteenth century.

"Station masters" in the Underground Railroad provided runaways with food, clothing, and "stations" (shelter). Stations included homes and barns with hiding places, secret passageways, and tunnels. Fugitives often slept in small crawl spaces between the floors of a house, in feeding troughs in barns, or at the bottom of covered wagons.

Robinson also taught her students about the people who worked hard to oppose slavery. White Quakers went to jail for teaching enslaved people to read and write, and worked with free African Americans to run the Underground Railroad, a system of secret routes for those escaping bondage in the South and traveling north to freedom.

Before the Civil War, West Chester, Pennsylvania, was a major stop on the Eastern Line of the Underground Railroad. That route led north from slaveholding states to places like Philadelphia, where slavery was illegal. There were many Underground Railroad stations in and around West Chester, partly because it was home to a group of free African Americans dedicated to liberating their friends and relatives from the chains of slavery. These abolitionists worked side by side with local Quakers to ensure that the Eastern Line was a safe route for those escaping slavery.

Robinson took her students on field trips to old Quaker houses that had once served as stations on the Underground Railroad. With Robinson as their guide, Bayard and his fellow students could see and touch the cramped spots where runaways had hidden from their owners and "slave catchers" intent on returning them South.

William Still was an Underground Railroad conductor. He wrote in his 1872 book, *The Underground Railroad*, "Many fugitives were indebted to Friends who aided them in a quiet way . . . and the result was that Underground Railroad operations were always pretty safe and prosperous where the line of travel led through 'Quaker settlements.'"[9]

Historically, West Chester was an important part of the Underground Railroad, but that did not mean the whole town supported the work of the abolitionists. Some local leaders believed black people were inferior to white people. To prevent the races from mixing, they enforced a system of racial segregation. African Americans were not allowed to sit with white people at local theaters, eat in certain restaurants, or use public restrooms in the center

Gay Street Elementary School was a "colored" school.

of town. Some buildings even had *whites only* signs on them. Black children, including Bayard, could not attend white public elementary schools.

Bayard's favorite teacher at Gay Street Elementary School was Maria Brock, the daughter of the pastor of the Rustins' church. She taught English and elocution and had a distinctive pattern of speech. Inspired by Brock, Bayard began speaking in an exact, sophisticated way, almost as if he was a member of royalty. As one of Bayard's fellow students at Gay Street remembered, "He would always be saying 'cahn't' when the rest of us were saying 'cain't.'"[10] Later in his life, people sometimes mistakenly thought he had gotten his accent from England or the Caribbean.

Brock told her students about the Harlem Renaissance. Many African Americans who migrated from the South settled in Harlem, a neighborhood in New York City. In the 1920s, Harlem was home to a vibrant community of African American writers, actors, musicians, and dancers. Their artistic accomplishments were known across the world. Brock's lessons about Harlem inspired Bayard to dream of living an exotic life far beyond West Chester. When reflecting on Brock later in life, Bayard said: "She not only stimulated in me a great desire to learn but also introduced me to the possibilities that education had for liberating one from the prison of inherited circumstances."[11]

17

Bayard at 16.

chapter 4

A DETERMINATION TO BE THE BEST

Although the elementary schools in West Chester were segregated, West Chester High School was integrated. Local white leaders thought it was too expensive to build and maintain a separate high school for the number of African American students who would attend. Many of them dropped out during their first or second year. To them, high school seemed futile as they imagined a future in which their academic work was not likely to lead to a successful career in West Chester, where prejudice and discrimination continued to favor white people over black people.

But Bayard did not drop out. He was "different," according to one of his classmates. "He had ambition and a great feeling about possibility. His determination was extraordinary. He had to prove that he was inferior to no one. He had to do what anybody said he couldn't do."[12]

Bayard continued his outstanding academic work at West Chester High School. Gifted with natural intelligence,

> " . . . A voice deep in my soul
> Urges me on,—and I will heed its call.
> Courage I have and strength for something better,
> Something far nobler than this present life . . ."
>
> — Henrik Ibsen, Catiline

Bayard won the boys' singles tennis championship at West Chester High School. A childhood friend recalled that Bayard cut a striking figure in his tennis whites, and that the girls in his neighborhood used to love watching him walk by their homes.

Bayard worked hard at his studies, earning a place in a program that focused on literature, language, and mathematics. It was unusual for African American students to be enrolled in a "college prep" program, but it was right where Bayard belonged—among other top students.

Bayard also had an artistic side. He acted in leading roles in several school productions, including *Catiline*, Henrik Ibsen's play about a first-century Roman politician who sought to overthrow aristocratic authorities.

Bayard's passion for the arts centered on vocal music. Gifted with a beautiful tenor voice, he sang in the choir at Bethel AME

The West Chester Warriors football team had an undefeated season in Bayard's senior year. Bayard is in the front row, third from the right.

Church and in a gospel quartet that performed locally. He developed his vocal technique under the direction of Floyd Hart, the music instructor and choirmaster at West Chester High School. Because Hart focused on classical music, Bayard learned to perform music by Bach, Schubert, and Brahms.

Bayard appreciated the opportunity to sing classical music, believing that it stretched his singing abilities in new and challenging ways. True to his resilient personality, he also relished the chance to surprise audiences who expected African Americans to sing only spirituals or the blues. Bayard certainly succeeded in surprising his fellow students when he performed an aria—in Italian—from an opera by Gaetano Donizetti in a high school assembly.

The versatile singer also excelled in public speaking. In his first year, he became the first African American student at West Chester High School to win a distinguished oratory contest, surely making Maria Brock proud of her former elocution student. The following year, his essay won first place in a writing contest.

Bayard's friends recognized his athletic abilities and encouraged him to try out for the high school football team. He became the team's starting left tackle and by his junior year he was selected as one of the best linemen in Chester County. A friend recalled that Bayard was "the toughest hitter on the front line. I wouldn't have expected that of a young man whose grandmother was raising him to be nonviolent."[13]

21

Bayard (front row, fourth from left) was a key part of the track team and helped set a state record for the mile relay.

Bayard ran in a wide variety of circles in high school, refusing to be limited to one or two predictable cliques. In addition to playing on the basketball, football, track, and tennis teams, he was a member of the science and French clubs, the history and drama clubs, the glee club and chorus. He was also elected to student government. Bayard would not stay in one place; nor would he keep his interests separate. Classmate John Rodgers remembered Bayard in a scrimmage football game: "Sometimes, after knocking me down on my face, he would gently help me to my feet and recite a line or two of poetry."[14]

Ironically, it was when he started at the integrated high school that Bayard really began to feel the effects of segregation. The segregation at Gay Street Elementary School had not seemed to bother Bayard, since there were many activities outside of school that included both black and white children, such as story time at the public library. Once he was in high school, though, he began to notice the discrimination that surrounded him.

It was customary at the time for students to develop close friendships only with members of their own race or ethnic group. Bayard refused to let social custom decide who his friends could be. His friendships with white classmates were not much of a problem at school, but things were different beyond the school walls. He was not allowed to sit with his white friends in the movies or restaurants. He was not allowed to play basketball with his white friends at the YMCA. He was not allowed to visit some of his white friends in their homes. He was not allowed to use the bathrooms in the shops and restaurants in town, as his white friends did; he had to run home to use the toilet.

Bayard's best friend in high school was John Cessna, a white student. The two shared common interests—running, writing, public speaking, and acting—and spent much of their time in the public library, one of the few places outside of school in West Chester where white and black students could sit together. Bayard and Cessna encountered prejudice from those unaccustomed to seeing races mix socially. Their fellow students called them "whitey" and "blackey," and Cessna's family refused to welcome Bayard into their home.

When Cessna learned that the local YMCA would not allow Bayard to join him there for winter track practices, he held his own personal sit-in at the director's office. That brave act did not change the policy, but it certainly cemented the friendship of the interracial pair.

Bayard also developed a reputation for resisting racial discrimination. He refused to accept racially segregated accommodations during an overnight trip to a state track meet in Altoona, Pennsylvania. Bayard and two other talented African American members of the track team, Charles Porter and Charlie Melton, told their coach that unless they were permitted to stay in the same hotel as the rest of the team, they would not run in the meet. Under

Bayard enjoyed reading and writing poetry. He published several of his poems in the school magazine, *Garnet and White*. Here is one titled *Cupid's Winter Message*.

Before me lies a curious sight—

A mass of Cupid's lace so bright,

A scarlet heart it seems to me—

I wonder what its purpose be?

I see its trees;
I feel its breeze
I stop to see,
Who thinks of me.

Ah! some fair one has sent it here

To tell her heart of love is near,

For Valentines are songs we sing

When Cupid's darts can't wait 'till spring.[17]

The Warner Theater, with its Art Deco style and 1,650 plush seats, opened for business while Bayard was in high school. Its managers directed African Americans to seats in the balcony, preventing them from sitting among white people on the main floor.

pressure, the coach agreed to the demand, although he was not pleased with the student protesters.

Bayard's identity as an activist grew when fellow students learned that he had sat in the *whites only* section at the local Warner Theater. When the police heard that Bayard was daring to sit where he was not allowed, they sped to the theater, arrested him, and took him to jail. It was the first of many arrests prompted by his protests against racial injustice.

His classmates chose Bayard to be one of six speakers at the West Chester High School graduation ceremony. It was obvious to Bayard's fellow students that the school's yearbook editors were exactly right in their assessment of him: "Yes, a hero on many a field, rising to the sublime in all because of a determination to be the best and to give the best."[15]

Graduation Day in June 1932 was a momentous occasion for Bayard. Standing tall in his dark jacket and white pants, he spoke about the ability of music "to lift one out of the fatigue and monotony of everyday life."[16] He punctuated his speech with a song for his fellow graduates and their families. The special day also saw Bayard earning recognition for his excellence in sports and academics.

But Graduation Day was also bittersweet. While Bayard's best friend John Cessna, also a commencement speaker, had plans to attend the University of Pennsylvania, Bayard saw no clear path ahead for himself. Although he had excelled in the classroom, earning more "honor points" than any other graduating senior, he did not receive any scholarship money from local authorities. Julia and Janifer were full of love for Bayard, but their bank account did not hold enough money to send him to college.

Complicating matters was the Great Depression; the country's economy was in shambles, and jobs with decent wages were scarce, leaving many people stuck in poverty. Bayard grew disappointed and discouraged. Maria Brock had taught him long ago that education could help him escape from "the prison of inherited circumstances," but he could no longer see any evidence that she was right. Despite his best efforts, racial prejudice seemed to be defining his future.

Julia Rustin, however, was not so sure. Because she had already encountered so many obstacles in her life, Bayard's grandmother had developed a keen sense of seeing a way to overcome them. In the summer following graduation, she put on her nicest dress and hat, marched up the steps leading to businesses and churches, and started knocking on doors. Bayard's biggest fan, a relentless "dealer in relieving misery," would not let her talented grandson languish for long.

When Bayard graduated from high school at age 20, his future was uncertain.

chapter 5

WE WERE REBELLIOUS

Julia Rustin was convinced that her talented grandson deserved a college scholarship. Although Bayard's high school record was outstanding and Julia's persistence was unshakable, she could not find anyone to pay for his education and living expenses. But giving up was not an option.

Ultimately, it was not his academic record that opened up a way for Bayard to go to college; it was his voice, his gorgeous tenor voice.

Bayard's singing impressed Bishop R.R. Wright, a wealthy minister at an AME church in Philadelphia and incoming president of Wilberforce University, a college for African Americans that was owned by the AME Church. With some urging from Julia, Wright offered Bayard a music scholarship.

In September of 1932, Bayard left West Chester for Wilberforce University in Xenia, Ohio, nearly five hundred miles away. He became a leading student in the music program, joining the chorus and a quartet of highly accomplished singers. With Bayard as its main tenor and soloist, the Wilberforce Quartet performed up and down the East Coast, from New York to the Deep South, singing to raise money for the university.

As Bayard became friends with African Americans from the

Deep South at Wilberforce, he was captivated by their extensive knowledge of African American cultural history, especially musical genres known as work songs and the blues. Unlike spirituals, with lyrics that focused on God and heaven, work songs and the blues addressed such things as shucking corn, roasting pigs, and longing for families and love. These songs expressed the everyday frustrations of African Americans working and living in the South, who wanted a better life here on earth, not just in heaven.

Bayard and his fellow singers added work songs and the blues to the Wilberforce Quartet's selections. This did not please the leaders of the AME Church at Wilberforce. "But we were rebellious," Bayard recalled. "Although we were scholarship students, we said to the church leadership, 'You may be paying our way, but we're still independent.'"[18] Bayard, it turns out, had not left his activist personality back in West Chester, and he and his friends continued to sing work songs and the blues, in addition to the spirituals, while performing in public.

Bayard was responsible for introducing the quartet's songs during public performances, and he believed that this experience provided him with "a great sense of how to present myself as a speaker. The Wilberforce Quartet gave me status and a greater self-assurance."[19] These public speaking skills would serve him well later in life.

Although Bayard participated enthusiastically in the music program at Wilberforce, he objected to the military training that was required of all male students. Wilberforce's Reserve Officer Training Corps (ROTC) program taught students how to fire rifles and become combat soldiers. Unlike the pacifist Quakers, the AME Church was not opposed to war and many members had served as soldiers in the Union Army during the Civil War and in the US Army during World War I. Although Bayard had attended the AME Church in West Chester, Julia's Quaker influence was strong. As a committed pacifist opposed to war preparations, Bayard resisted the ROTC requirement.

Some say he lost his scholarship because he refused to join ROTC. Others say he had not found the coursework at Wilberforce to be challenging enough for him. In later years, Bayard also claimed that university administrators asked him to leave campus after he organized a student protest against the poor quality of the food in the college cafeteria.

Whatever the reason, Bayard left Wilberforce University after little more than a year, but during that year he had learned something very important about himself. He was becoming aware that he was physically and emotionally attracted to men.

At the time, psychologists considered homosexuality to be a mental illness. The government labeled gay men as security risks and would not hire someone they knew to be homosexual, feeling that the stigma against them could be a tool for blackmailers seeking government secrets. Many religious people considered homosexuality to be a sin. Gay people were routinely fired from their jobs, harassed, and discriminated against in other ways. Such discrimination was permitted, if not encouraged. In fact, up until 1962, homosexuality was a crime in every state. Same-sex couples could even be arrested for dancing or holding hands with each other. Most homosexuals remained hidden "in the closet," and were not public about their sexual orientation.

But Bayard did not consider his sexual orientation to be sick, sinful, or criminal. He accepted it as a natural part of his personality and refused to hide it or feel ashamed about it. He was grateful that the most important person in his life, his grandmother Julia, did not belittle or condemn his attraction to men. While they never talked about his sexual orientation in any detail, Julia encouraged Bayard to be himself and to bring his male friends to dinner at the Rustin home in West Chester. Her concern was not that Bayard dated men; she just wanted him be careful about the men he chose to spend time with. Julia's warmth and support gave Bayard great comfort. Years later he said, "I think that a family in which the members know and accept one's lifestyle is the most helpful factor for emotional stability."[20]

However confident he might have been in his developing identity and abilities, Bayard was not so sure about his future. The Great Depression continued, and jobs were scarce, so Bayard went home to West Chester, where a warm meal, a comfortable bed, and a sense of belonging were always available to him.

By the fall of 1934 he was enrolled as a student at Cheyney State Teachers College, a few miles away from his home. Once again, it

The American Friends Service Committee (AFSC)

AFSC was founded in 1917, during World War I, as an alternative to military service for pacifists. Young AFSC volunteers drove ambulances in the war zone in France and helped get food and clothing to people in need. After the war, AFSC expanded its mission to help people affected by war, feeding children and aiding refugees. AFSC continues to work for peace and justice around the world. In 1947, AFSC and a group of British Quakers accepted the Nobel Peace Prize on behalf of Quakers worldwide.

was his voice that paid his way to college. Cheyney's new president, Dr. Leslie Pinckney Hill, had offered him a music scholarship.

Bayard became a valuable member of the Cheyney State Quartet, performing in Pennsylvania and neighboring states. He even sang solos on Philadelphia radio stations, and the college newspaper described him as a "gifted and popular tenor soloist."[21]

Like Wilberforce, Cheyney was established to educate African American students. Bayard enjoyed his new school. He was especially pleased that Cheyney, which was founded by Quakers in 1837, did not require its students to participate in military training. Freed from firing rifles and learning the ways of combat, he could focus on Quaker spirituality, observing daily periods of quiet contemplation, and delving more deeply into Quaker beliefs about human dignity, the unity of the human family, and nonviolence. He became even more convinced of the values he had learned from Julia as a child and, though he was raised in the AME Church, he considered himself a Quaker. He drew strength from his Quaker beliefs.

By now it was becoming clear that war was on the horizon. Hitler was gaining power in Germany, Italy had invaded Ethiopia, and Japan was becoming aggressive toward other countries in Asia. As a Quaker and a member of Cheyney's Debating Society, Bayard devoted considerable time to debating the meaning of pacifism for the wider world. In 1937, he also had the opportunity to take part in a major educational conference when Cheyney hosted the Institute of International Relations. Sponsored by a Quaker group called the American Friends Service Committee (AFSC), the institute brought

Bayard at AFSC training camp.

three hundred college students, professors, and peace activists from across the country together on the Cheyney campus to debate the causes of war and to find ways to prevent it.

With financial help from Cheyney, Bayard continued his association with the AFSC by joining a student peace brigade in the summer of 1937. Bayard and three other peace brigade members moved into the YMCA in Auburn, New York. They met with community leaders and taught local residents about peace and nonviolence. Bayard also sang about peace on the local radio station, helped lead peace programs at a playground, and even produced a youth ballet about peace. This work with the Quakers marked the beginning of his lifelong efforts to build peace in local communities and across the globe.

Unfortunately, racial prejudice remained constant in his life. No matter where he went, he experienced discrimination because of his skin color. Bayard felt this acutely when he and his fellow brigade member, Robert Bilheimer, stopped to have lunch with

Robert's father, a YMCA executive in New York City, at the end of the summer. After Robert's father met Bayard in the lobby of the YMCA, he took his son aside and told him that because Bayard was African American he could not eat in the main cafeteria. Robert's father was visibly upset and disappeared upstairs for a while. Upon returning, he escorted his son and Bayard to a private room—a segregated room—set up just for their lunch. "I was mortified," Robert recalled. "Bayard kept up a fine conversation, saying nothing about the situation. At the end, he thanked my father and took his leave of us. I knew him well enough to know that he must have been outraged. But he clearly understood my mortification, and he was willing to leave it at that."[22]

Back at Cheyney, Bayard prepared for his last year of coursework. Graduation was just around the corner, and he seemed to have a promising future as a well-known performer and a first-rate music teacher. But then Bayard did something that caused President Hill to call him into his office. He would never tell a historian or an interviewer what he had done, but it was serious enough for President Hill to expel him from the school. Bayard left campus in the fall of 1937 and went back to live with Julia and Janifer in West Chester. Unable to find a suitable job in West Chester or Philadelphia, Bayard set his sights on New York City.

A flyer issued by the American Friends Service Committee urging international cooperation instead of war.

HUNDREDS ARE RECEIVING

FREE INSTRUCTION

DRAWING·PAINTING·WEAVING
LITHOGRAPHY·SCULPTURE·ETCHING
METAL CRAFT·PHOTOGRAPHY
COSTUME ILLUSTRATION

HARLEM COMMUNITY ART CENTER
290 LENOX AVE·NEW YORK NY

FEDERAL ART PROJECT
WORKS PROGRESS ADMINISTRATION
235 EAST 42 STREET·NEW YORK NY

During the Great Depression, the Works Progress Administration (WPA) employed millions of people, including Bayard.

chapter 6

THE POWER OF NONVIOLENCE

To twenty-five-year-old Bayard Rustin, Harlem was a world away from West Chester. This neighborhood of New York City was a vibrant place where African American musicians, actors, dancers, poets, and novelists lived, worked, and played. Cars and streetcars rushed by as Bayard walked along 125th Street, past cafes, dance halls, and theaters. Community activists handed out literature or stood on wooden soapboxes, giving speeches that demanded more jobs and better housing. Bayard often chatted with these "soapbox orators" about politics and economics.

Harlem was home to a community of artists and activists—black and white, gay and straight. There were Quakers in New York, too. Bayard made New York his home for the rest of his life.

Bayard stayed with his Aunt Bessie, a public school teacher, until he could afford a place of his own. He found a job with the Works Progress Administration (WPA), a government agency that created jobs for millions of people during the Great Depression. For two years under the WPA, Bayard worked as a high school English teacher and as a youth center director. He also filled in for singers at the world-famous Apollo Theater on 125th Street when scheduled performers were absent.

Once again, Bayard's voice opened doors for him. He was invited to join the chorus of the musical *John Henry*, which was to open on Broadway on January 10, 1940. Bayard was thrilled. Not only would he be paid to sing on Broadway, but the all-black musical starred Paul Robeson, a famous singer and actor known for his outspoken efforts to advance civil rights for African Americans.

Unfortunately, *John Henry* flopped, lasting on Broadway for only five performances. But Bayard's tenor voice had caught the attention of Josh White, a blues singer featured in the musical, who asked Bayard to join his group, Josh White and the Carolinians. Bayard agreed, of course, and the quintet performed in nightclubs around the city—white, black, and integrated clubs—especially in Greenwich Village, a neighborhood that was home to many artists, musicians, and writers. Columbia Records produced and distributed the quintet's album, *Chain Gang*.

Besides sharing a love for the blues, Bayard and Josh White were both interested in fighting social injustice, and they were attracted to a political and social movement called communism. Communists were prominent among those speaking on 125th Street, demanding economic justice and civil rights for African Americans. Bayard joined the Young Communist League (YCL) to help in the fight against racial discrimination and poverty. As an active YCL member, he became one of Harlem's soapbox orators, giving fiery speeches about the need for jobs and freedom.

He enrolled at the City College of New York, taking free classes, talking to other students about race and justice, and inviting them to YCL meetings where they made plans to spread their message throughout the city. As a student organizer, he gained skills that would serve him well in years to come. Bayard was such a good organizer that YCL leaders asked him to establish YCL groups on college campuses all over the state.

Bayard's work with the YCL attracted the attention of the Federal Bureau of Investigation (FBI). The FBI spied on communists, who were considered threats to the United States government, and began to investigate Bayard, asking his neighbors about his comings and goings. An FBI agent even tried to interview Bayard, but Bayard would have none of it. He met the agent in the hallway of his apartment building. In the spirit of Quaker openness and truth, he announced so that other residents could hear, "This is an FBI man. He's here to question me. I refuse to say anything to him. I will have no relationship with him whatsoever. You are free to tell him whatever you want, but I just want you to know who he is and what his purpose is."[23] That was the last Bayard saw of that FBI agent.

In early 1941, the Young Communist League gave Bayard a leading role in a campaign to desegregate the US military. The military recruited African Americans to fight, but denied them the freedom to live and work alongside white soldiers. Bayard was enthusiastic about combating racial segregation in the military, and agreed with the YCL's opposition to the war in Europe.

When Nazi Germany invaded the Soviet Union in June of 1941, Bayard's life took a new direction. Communist leaders in New York, confronted with the threat of Hitler, decided that desegregating the US military was less important than supporting the war and assisting the communist Soviet Union. Bayard was shocked at the YCL's demand that he stop the campaign against a segregated military, and he realized that "the communists' primary concern was not with the black masses but with the global objectives of the Soviet Union."[24] Disillusioned, Bayard left the YCL. For the rest of his life he remained critical of countries that embraced communism at the expense of freedom, equality, and human rights.

Determined to continue his fight against racial segregation, Bayard arranged to meet with A. Philip Randolph, the founder and president of the Brotherhood of Sleeping Car Porters, the nation's largest union of African American workers. Randolph was already a respected member of the civil rights community. A bold thinker who was also committed to nonviolent mass action, Randolph was drawing up plans for thousands of African Americans to march on Washington to protest their exclusion from jobs in factories that

March on Washington Community Bookshop and Headquarters.

produced weapons and ammunition. Both Randolph and Bayard were anti-war, but they understood that there were many jobs for unskilled workers in the factories supplying the European war effort—jobs that should have been open to all, not reserved for white workers only.

Bayard joined the March on Washington Movement (MOWM) as an organizer, but his help was not needed for long. Faced with the possibility of a massive march of African American people on the nation's capital, President Franklin D. Roosevelt hastily issued an executive order stating "there shall be no discrimination in the employment of workers in defense industries or government because of race, creed, color, or national origin."[25]

With victory in hand, Randolph called off the march.

Although the MOWM remained active, it did not require Bayard's full-time effort. A.J. Muste, an internationally known pacifist and labor activist, recruited Bayard to join the staff of an interfaith peace organization called the Fellowship of Reconciliation (FOR). Muste

Gandhi

Mohandas Gandhi was born in India in 1869. (Later in his life he was called *Mahatma*, which means "Great Soul," out of respect.) He studied law in England, and then lived in South Africa for 20 years, where he fought discrimination against Indians in that country and developed his concept of nonviolent direct action.

In 1914, he returned to India, which was a British colony at the time. Gandhi became a leader in the struggle for Indian independence. His nonviolent direct action campaigns included marches, rallies, boycotts, and strikes. Gandhi was arrested many times, and his followers were often beaten mercilessly or even killed.

In 1947, after 27 years of struggle, India won its independence.

Bayard with A.J. Muste. After learning of Bayard's commitment to Quaker pacifism, his speaking and singing abilities, and his experience in educating and organizing, Muste hired him to join the Fellowship of Reconciliation (FOR) staff.

The Power of Nonviolence

Richard B. Gregg, a Quaker lawyer, and his book, *The Power of Nonviolence*, had a great influence on Bayard and the FOR. Gregg lived in India for four years, spending seven months in Gandhi's *ashram* community. His book described the psychology of nonviolent resistance and offered advice for interested groups.

As Gregg described it, if a protester is attacked and fights back, the attacker feels justified in using more violence. But if a protester responds to physical violence calmly, without fear or anger, and without fighting back, it throws the attacker off balance. The attacker is surprised and confused, not sure what to do. By not fighting back, the nonviolent protester shows that his belief in the cause is strong, and that he respects the humanity of every person—even his attacker. The attacker uses a lot of energy and starts to feel uncomfortable, especially if there are witnesses.

The purpose of nonviolent resistance is not to defeat or humiliate the attacker but to convince the attacker that violence does not work and that they can solve the problem by working together.

was a great admirer of Mohandas Gandhi and the nonviolent campaigns he was waging to liberate India from British colonial rule.

As the new head of the FOR, Muste wanted to build a staff of young Gandhians committed to using both education and direct action campaigns to spread the message of peace across the United States. Bayard loved his new job as youth secretary, traveling around the country and speaking at high schools, colleges, youth conferences, and churches. He educated young people about the philosophy of nonviolence, trained them in direct action tactics, and organized them in local groups committed to peace and justice.

On December 7, 1941, Japanese warplanes attacked a United States naval base at Pearl Harbor, Hawaii, killing 2,400 Americans. War was no longer a distant rumble an ocean away. The United States officially entered World War II, fighting alongside Great Britain and the Soviet Union against Germany, Italy, and Japan. Now that the country was at war, Bayard was even more determined to work for peace.

Library of Congress, United States Navy

After the Japanese attack on Pearl Harbor, the United States entered World War II.

While working for the Fellowship of Reconciliation, Bayard taught young people about nonviolent direct action.

NONVIOLENT DIRECT ACTION

On a hot day in 1942, Bayard traveled by bus from Louisville, Kentucky to Nashville, Tennessee, for one of his speaking engagements. As he boarded a bus in Louisville, a young white boy in his mother's lap reached out and grabbed Bayard's red tie as he passed by. The mother hit her son, saying, "Don't touch a n*****." Bayard was shocked. "I had not seen this kind of thing before," he remembered, "so I went in the back and sat down and I began doodling in the back seat by myself, and all of a sudden something began to happen."

As he recalled the mother's hurtful actions, Bayard wondered "how many years are we going to let that child be misled by its mother?" If black people accepted the racially segregated seating patterns in buses, the child would never learn that racial segregation was wrong. "I vowed then and there," Bayard recalled, "I was never going through the South again without either being arrested or thrown off the bus or protesting."[26]

Suddenly inspired, Bayard rose from his seat and moved to the *whites only* section. The driver told Bayard to move back. "My friend," Bayard replied. "I believe that is an unjust law. If I were to sit in back I would be condoning injustice."

The driver called the police, but Bayard would not budge. Even when the police arrived, he refused to move. The police beat him, dragged him off the bus, threw him on the ground, and kicked him. Using his training in nonviolence, Bayard didn't move, but let them kick him again and again. Then he stood up and said, "There is no need to beat me. I am not resisting you."

As the other bus passengers looked on, the police put Bayard in the back of a police car and continued to kick him and call him names, trying to make him fight back, but Bayard stayed calm. At the police station they pummeled him again, even ripping his clothes as they tossed him back and forth to one another. Bayard showed no fear—at least on the outside. "I am fortified by truth, justice, and Christ," he said. "There is no need for me to fear."[27]

Bayard's lack of resistance baffled the police—one officer called him "crazy"—but it had inspired one of the white bus riders to visit the police station and seek Bayard's release. The assistant district attorney questioned Bayard for half an hour and decided not to press charges, saying, "You may go, *Mister* Rustin."[28]

After this incident, Bayard was even more convinced of the power of nonviolence to fight racial injustice. He had been released, a white bus rider had come to help him, and the district attorney had addressed him as *Mister* Rustin. White Southerners almost never addressed African American men as *Mister*.

Bayard continued to travel and teach with the FOR and with A. Philip Randolph's March on Washington Movement. He taught small groups of students to use Gandhian tactics to fight racial segregation. He preached peace and nonviolence to conference audiences of thousands. He organized local groups to use nonviolent direct action to fight discrimination and to pressure the government to protect the civil rights of African Americans. Fearing that some African Americans would resort to violence in their quest for freedom and equality, Bayard believed it was FOR's responsibility "to put the technique of nonviolent direct action into the hands of the black masses."[29] His audiences were eager to find out about Gandhi, who was stirring things up in India with civil disobedience in the struggle to win independence from Great Britain.

At the same time, Bayard sought to change the prejudiced attitudes held by many white people in his audiences. Sometimes his tactics were simple, but effective. While on his first speaking tour,

War Without Violence

Bayard and the FOR learned about Gandhi's methods from Krishnalal Shridharani, who worked with Gandhi in India and wrote a book called *War Without Violence*. Shridharani explained Gandhi's philosophy of nonviolent direct action, or *satyagraha*, which translates as "insistence on the truth."

When Gandhi was working toward independence for India, he started by negotiating for changes in the laws. If that was not successful, he began "agitating," or educating people about the problem. The movement would then spread by "social contagion" and result in larger and larger demonstrations. He would then *demand* change. If change still did not occur, Gandhi and his followers would use nonviolent tactics including protests, boycotts, and civil disobedience

Interracial Primer

As part of his work with the FOR, Bayard wrote a pamphlet, *Interracial Primer: How You Can Help Relieve Tension Between Negroes and Whites.* It explained some of the reasons for interracial tensions and offered practical ways to reduce that tension, such as:

• Subscribe to periodicals published by or concerning the Negro.

• Form an interracial group to study some common problems other than racial issues.

• Explode racial misconceptions. Be fortified with facts such as . . . Scientifically there is no difference between Negro and white blood plasma.

• Encourage local public schools to include accounts of valiant and heroic Negroes in the . . . history courses.

• Urge local papers not to accept job . . . advertisements specifying 'white' or 'Christian.'

• Avoid 'funny' and offensive stories concerning Negroes.

• Urge your congressman to . . . vote for one of the seven anti-lynching bills presented to the new Congress.

• Work to abolish racial discrimination and segregation in your church.[33]

he sat quietly in a pew at an Ohio church while his hosts huddled together at the start of the meeting, waiting for their scheduled speaker, Bayard Rustin. One of the hosts said, "Why don't we ask the Negro janitor sitting back there if he has seen the speaker in any part of the building." Bayard replied, "I am Bayard Rustin." Years later, one of the hosts recalled: "We had never known many black people, and never dreamed that Bayard Rustin would be black. Well, we learned a lot that night," about peace and racial prejudice. "We would never be the same again."[30]

African Americans were not the only targets of racial discrimination. Because Japan had attacked Pearl Harbor, Japanese immigrants and their American-born children were viewed by many with fear and suspicion, particularly on the West Coast. The government confiscated the homes and businesses of Japanese Americans and forced them to go to inland internment camps. Over 100,000 people were sent to the camps, most of them American citizens.

Organizations that opposed war and racial injustice, including the FOR and the AFSC, sent workers to help support the people in camps and to protect the property they left behind. Bayard, who had worked with both groups, was an ideal candidate to visit the camps and report on conditions there.

Bayard believed that all races and nationalities—and even "the enemy"—were part of the human family. During his travels, Bayard encountered German prisoners being transported on a train through Texas. The military police (MP) escorting the prisoners arranged for them to eat in the train's dining car before the rest of the civilian passengers. An American woman took offense at this, believing that it showed preference for the Germans, and she slapped a German soldier in the face. Bayard witnessed the assault and, because of his Quaker conviction that everyone should be treated with dignity and respect, encouraged the woman to apologize. After she refused, he asked the MPs if he could speak with the soldiers. But they said they were not permitted to let a civilian speak with prisoners of war. So Bayard said: "Is there a regulation saying that I cannot sing to them?" The MPs knew of no such rule, so Bayard sang two songs for the prisoners, including one called "A Stranger in a Distant Land." The soldier who had been slapped put his arm around Bayard and mustered enough English to say, "I thank you."[31]

Bayard still believed what he had said in high school—that music could "lift one out of the fatigue and monotony of everyday life." He often concluded his speaking engagements by quieting his audience, standing still in the middle of the stage, placing his hands behind his back, and singing deeply moving spirituals and ballads.

In his years with the MOWM and the FOR, Bayard matured in his role as a political speaker and organizer. His appearance and personality added to his effectiveness—tall, handsome, charming, eloquent, with a voice that captivated the men and women in the audience. He inspired strangers to become peace and civil rights activists, to build interracial coalitions, and to raise the money required to wage campaigns for peace and racial justice in both the streets and the courts.

One person was particularly enchanted with Bayard. Davis Platt, a young white man, met Bayard at Bryn Mawr College, near Philadelphia, where Bayard had come to speak. As Platt recalled, "The moment our eyes met it was electric."[32]

Bayard was confident in his sexual identity and lived as an openly gay man. He and Platt began a long-term relationship. Platt moved to New York City so they could be closer, but they would soon be separated, and Bayard's life was about to change dramatically.

Members of an African American artillery unit in Belgium during World War II.

WAR IS WRONG

In 1940, while war was raging overseas, the US government passed a law requiring all men aged 21 to 35 to register with the draft board. At that time they were not required to serve in the military, only to register. Just in case. Men with a religious objection to serving in the military could register as conscientious objectors (COs). Instead of fighting, COs could work in a military job that did not use weapons or work at a Civilian Public Service (CPS) camp.

In the fall of 1940, Bayard informed his local draft board that because of his commitment to Quaker pacifism, he wanted to be listed in the government's records as a CO. The board agreed to his request.

Civilian Public Service

If a man was a conscientious objector (CO), opposed on religious grounds to participating in the military, he could serve, without pay, in the Civilian Public Service (CPS), performing work of "national importance."[43] Eventually, there were 152 church-supported CPS camps across the country, where men performed work including soil conservation, forestry, and fire-fighting. Some worked as aides in psychiatric hospitals. Others became subjects of medical experiments, allowing themselves to be starved or to be intentionally infected with malaria or hepatitis.

> "Quaker pacifism is an obligation, not a promise. We are not guaranteed that it will be safe. We are sure that it is right."
>
> – Friends Peace Committee, Philadelphia Yearly Meeting (Race Street), 1940[44]

After the attack on Pearl Harbor in 1941, the US entered the war and thousands of American men lined up to volunteer to fight. To increase the size of the military quickly, the government expanded the age range for registering to include men between the ages of 18 and 65. Men who were 18 to 45 years old could be called up to fight, whether they volunteered or not. If they refused to volunteer or submit to the draft, the government sent them to jail.

Bayard continued to travel and speak about nonviolence, peace, and justice. He also advised young men to refuse military service in World War II, even though it meant they could go to jail. After traveling to twenty states and covering over ten thousand miles, he said, "I believe this is the time to say louder and more frequently that war is wrong, stupid, wasteful, and impeding future progress."[34]

In the years he spent traveling around the country, Bayard came to believe that it was wrong for pacifists to give any kind of support to the war effort. Indirect assistance, such as working in a CPS camp, was wrong, too. To cooperate with any of the government's laws about war, he now believed, was to support the war effort—something he must never do as a Quaker who believed that war mocked "the basic spiritual truth that men are brothers in the sight of God."

On November 13, 1943, Bayard received a letter ordering him to report for a physical examination and begin his service in a CPS camp. By that time, his opposition to war was even stronger than it had been in 1940, when he was granted CO status. He sent a letter to the draft board explaining that war was wrong, the draft was wrong, and that it was wrong to separate Americans from Germans or Japanese, or black soldiers from white soldiers. "That which separates man from his brother is evil and must be resisted."[35] He also informed them of his intent to break the law by not reporting for his physical.

Bayard was arrested on January 12, 1944, but he remained confident in his decision, believing it to be a Gandhian act of civil disobedience—open defiance of an unjust law. Like Gandhi, Bayard did not seek to evade arrest; he waived his right to a trial and pled guilty to breaking the law. Also like Gandhi, he did not try to avoid punishment when a federal judge sentenced him to three years in federal prison. Ten days after receiving his sentence, Bayard reported to a federal detention facility on West Street in Manhattan.

Bayard got started with civil disobedience right away. Just two days after he arrived at West Street, the jailers described him as "very troublesome." Bayard refused to sit at racially segregated tables in the jail's dining hall. He visited the jail's

Bayard arrived at Ashland on March 9, 1944, eight days before his thirty-second birthday. It did not take long for him to become the unofficial leader of the COs at Ashland.

business office when he was not allowed to be there and "became obstinate when ordered to go to his cell."[36]

After ten days, he was transferred to Ashland Federal Correction Institution in Kentucky. Upon arriving at the prison, he was unhappy to discover segregation virtually everywhere—in the cafeteria, common rooms, entertainment areas, even the jail cells—and quickly arranged to meet with the prison's senior official, Warden R.P. Hagerman, to discuss the troubling situation.

After their talk, Bayard wrote a letter to the warden about racial discrimination in prison. It was a remarkably bold move for a young black man in a Southern prison.

"There are four ways in which one can deal with an injustice," he wrote:

(a) One can accept it without protest.

(b) One can seek to avoid it.

(c) One can resist the injustice nonviolently.

(d) One can resist by violence.[37]

51

Library of Congress, Harris and Ewing, photographer

James Bennett, director of the Bureau of Prisons in Washington, DC. Warden Hagerman complained to Bennett that Bayard was "an extremely capable agitator" and "a constant troublemaker," and asked him to transfer Bayard to another federal prison. Bennett refused.

By the time he finished reading the letter, Warden Hagerman must have known this young man from New York City had no interest in accepting or avoiding any of the racial injustices at Ashland. He was right: Bayard Rustin, prisoner number 2905, was a nonviolent resister.

Bayard began his campaign for racial integration by refusing to sit in a section reserved for African Americans in the movie theater.

His next target was the recreation room.

In Bayard's cellblock, black and white inmates were separated by floors; black prisoners lived on the lower level, and white prisoners on the upper level. Each level had its own recreation room. Bayard and a white friend, CO Charles Butcher, asked Warden Hagerman to allow prisoners of different races to intermingle in the recreation rooms. Hagerman agreed to test the idea.

Bayard was the only African American to visit the recreation room on the upper level, and his presence there did not please some of the white prisoners. One of them, Elam Huddleston, threatened to beat Bayard up if he ever saw him again in the recreation room.

The next time Bayard went to the white prisoners' recreation room, Huddleston made good on his threat. He grabbed a wooden stick and struck Bayard's head, collarbone, and wrist so hard that the stick—and Bayard's wrist—broke. Bayard's friends tried to stop the attack, but Bayard protested, insisting on nonviolence in the face of violence.

Warden Hagerman congratulated Bayard on his nonviolent response to Huddleston, which built "respect for Negroes and for the methods by which conscientious objectors face violence and try to win justice."[38] The warden added that he would consider integrating the cellblock where Bayard and Charles Butcher lived. Bayard was making progress.

In addition to his nonviolent resistance, Bayard kept himself busy in ways that helped the cause of racial integration. He taught history to a class of white prisoners. He shared his musical gifts with the other prisoners by directing an operetta for a racially integrated cast of 51 men. He even formed an interracial choir that performed music from European American and African American traditions in church services at the prison.

Bayard continued to develop his own musical talents. He taught himself to play the mandolin that Davis Platt had given him. Bayard and Platt had continued their relationship while Bayard was in prison. Because of the laws against homosexuality, when they wrote about their relationship in their letters, they often referred to Platt as *Marie*. Bayard wrote to Platt that his letters were "a kind of food for my spirit, which only seeing you could replace."[39]

His grandmother, Julia, also wrote him letters to bolster his spirit. She assured him that he was under God's care and that his family continued to love him dearly. She also wrote to Bayard's jailers, asking them to treat him well and reminding them that they would be answerable to God if they did not.[40]

Bayard's efforts at desegregating the prison started to produce results. The Protestant church service allowed black and white inmates to sit together. Black and white kitchen workers began sitting together. The athletic program saw black and white prisoners playing together.

The next step was to desegregate the dining room. Bayard asked Warden Hagerman for interracial seating in the dining room on a voluntary basis—for those who *wanted* to sit together. He also pressured Warden Hagerman to integrate the entire cellblock where he and Butcher lived.

Bayard's plans for integrating the dining room and living

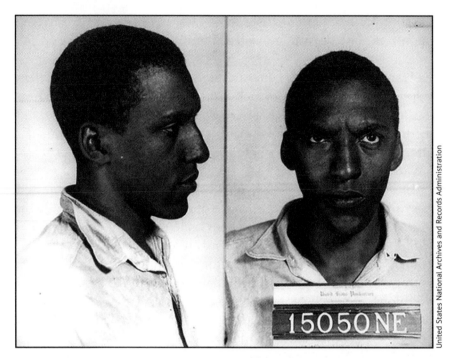

Bayard continued to struggle for racial integration at Lewisburg, even conducting a hunger strike, but he did not see any significant success.

quarters came to a screeching halt in the fall of 1944. Prison authorities claimed he had broken rules prohibiting physical affection between male prisoners. The prison guards put him in solitary confinement. Separated from his friends, Bayard could not follow through on any of his plans. With his campaign effectively shut down, Bayard found life very difficult for the next several months.

This turn of events did not please A.J. Muste, Bayard's supervisor at the Fellowship of Reconciliation (FOR), who felt that if word of Bayard's sexual orientation got out, it would endanger the Fellowship's work. He even encouraged Bayard to break up with Platt and consider a relationship with a woman, like Helen Winnemore, a Quaker activist who had fallen in love with Bayard. Bayard struggled with this, writing to Platt, "Emotionally, I am at present strongly attached to Marie [meaning Platt]; intellectually, I know that every effort must be made to find a different solution, for my vocation, which is my life, is at stake."[41] Bayard listened to his heart, not his head. His sexual orientation was part of his personality and he could not change who he was. He stayed with Platt. Muste was deeply disappointed.

Bayard's campaign for racial integration never recovered during his remaining time at Ashland prison. Nor did his ongoing efforts to desegregate ever enjoy the level of success he had achieved in his early days at Ashland. Bayard was eventually transferred to another prison, in Lewisburg, Pennsylvania.

Within a week after Bayard was transferred to Pennsylvania, events on the other side of the world would change the direction of Bayard's life again. US military planes dropped atomic bombs on two cities in Japan, instantly killing over 70,000 children, women, and men in Hiroshima and over 40,000 in Nagasaki. Pacifists across the world were horrified at the spectacle of atomic bombs killing so many civilians and leveling entire neighborhoods, including schools, homes, and places of worship. The surrender of Japan on September 3, 1945, brought an end to World War II.

Muste visited Bayard in prison shortly after the atomic bombings, encouraging him to seek early release from the prison by exhibiting good behavior. Bayard agreed, and the next day he informed Lewisburg's warden that he was abandoning his efforts to establish racial integration at the prison. "What does this mean?" he wrote in a letter to the warden. "It means that I now consider that I am needed on the outside to work among my people to call their attention to the great danger before us, for today the atomic bomb is an issue which means that we face total destruction if we do not find a way to peace."[42]

Bayard committed himself to good behavior, and on June 11, 1946, he walked out of Lewisburg prison a free man, more ready than ever to lead the world in a march toward peace.

"THE CHRISTIAN FAITH AND ATOMIC WARFARE"

Conference under the auspices of
THE AMERICAN FRIENDS SERVICE COMMITTEE

DR. EDDY ASIRVATHAM

Head of the International Relations
Department of the University of
Madras. Now teaching at Boston
University.

BAYARD RUSTIN

Secretary of the Fellowship of
Reconciliation.

SUNDAY, NOVEMBER 10, 1946

4:00 P.M. Address and Forum: "World Fellowship"
Dr. Asirvatham

Bayard Rustin will sing

6:00 P.M. Supper Conference: "Non-Violence"
Address by Bayard Rustin

8:00 P.M. Address by   "Christian Alternative to Atomic Warfare"
Dr. Asirvatham

Bayard Rustin will sing

ST. LUKE'S EVANGELICAL & REFORMED CHURCH

RICHMOND AVENUE AT W. UTICA STREET

Buffalo, New York

Supper: $1.00. Make reservations as early as possible by writing or 'phoning:

GRACE M. ALEXANDER

308 Summer Street

Telephone: Lincoln 3491

Admission to all sessions will be free. An offering will be taken for the work of the American Friends
Service Committee, Peace Section at the evening session.

Estate of Bayard Rustin

Bayard often sang at his speaking engagements.

chapter 9

"YOU DON'T HAVE TO RIDE JIM CROW"

Freed from prison, Bayard moved into an apartment in New York City with Davis Platt, where they lived together for about a year. When it became clear that the relationship would not last, they agreed to separate. Bayard returned to work at the FOR. His boss, A.J. Muste, sent him on a nationwide speaking tour and for the next several years, Bayard visited colleges, churches, and clubs, talking about the dangers of atomic warfare and the desperate need for building peace and racial harmony. The oratory skills he had learned in high school served him well. "You would see people with tears coming out of their eyes," recalled his friend and FOR coworker George Houser. "He could respond to a group or get in touch with them because he was a likable, creative personality."[45]

Speaking out against war was not enough for Bayard. Not long after the end of World War II, he wanted the FOR to undertake a massive direct action campaign against increasing US militarization. Although the FOR leadership was hesitant, Bayard organized public meetings calling for young men to burn their military service registration cards. He also began to plan the most important direct action campaign to date—against racial segregation on buses.

In 1942, Bayard had been beaten and arrested for sitting in the *whites only* section of a bus. Four years later, the US Supreme Court

Morgan v. Virginia

In July 1944, Irene Morgan, a 27-year-old African American woman, was traveling home to Baltimore, Maryland, on a Greyhound bus after visiting her mother in Virginia. When the bus became crowded, the driver insisted that Morgan surrender her seat to a white passenger. Morgan refused, and when a deputy sheriff tried to arrest her, she put up a fight. As she recalled the incident years later, "He put his hand on me to arrest me, so I took my foot and kicked him. . . . I started to bite him, but he looked dirty, so I couldn't bite him. So all I could do was claw and tear his clothes."[49]

Morgan pleaded guilty to resisting arrest, but she refused to pay the fine for violating Virginia's segregation laws. The NAACP provided her with an attorney, Thurgood Marshall, to appeal the fine in court. Her case went to the Supreme Court of the United States, and on June 3, 1946, eight days before Bayard left Lewisburg prison, the justices ruled it was unconstitutional for states to apply their segregation laws to passengers traveling from one state to another. Marshall, who would later become a Supreme Court justice, said, "Now is the time to push for the end of all forms of segregation throughout the country."[50]

ruled in *Morgan v. Virginia* that segregation on interstate buses was unconstitutional. But a court decision was one thing; actual desegregation was another. Would bus companies abide by the court's decision? Bayard Rustin and George Houser wanted to find out.

Bayard and Houser came up with a plan for an interracial group of men to ride buses throughout southern states. African American members of the group would ride in the front section (normally reserved for white passengers), and white members would ride either in the front or in the rear (reserved for black passengers). If bus drivers insisted that the black riders move to the rear of the bus, "[t]he Negro member will refuse to move to the rear when told to do so, and the white persons will support them. . . . In no case will the test group take any action tending toward violence."[46]

Bayard and Houser sent their proposal to African American leaders across the country. Most praised the idea, but Thurgood Marshall of the NAACP had doubts. Marshall, who had been Irene

Bayard and George Houser were good friends with similar dreams about racial justice, and they often worked together at the Fellowship of Reconciliation.

Morgan's lawyer, had experience as an African American attorney working for racial justice in the South. The year before, he was almost lynched by a mob of white men after he won an important case in Tennessee. Marshall warned Bayard and Houser against going to the Deep South, the most dangerous area of the South, and agitating white people who were already angry about African Americans exercising their constitutional rights. Marshall feared that the kind of actions Bayard and Houser were proposing would provoke violence by local authorities, "which would result in the imprisonment of hundreds of young people and the death of scores, with nothing achieved except a measure of publicity which we are now getting for our struggle with a minimum of suffering."[47]

Bayard and Houser revised their plans to avoid the Deep South (Alabama, Georgia, Louisiana, Mississippi, and South Carolina) and limit the trip to the Upper South (parts of Virginia, North Carolina, Tennessee, and Kentucky). Marshall eventually offered his endorsement of what would be called "The Journey of Reconciliation."

On April 9, 1947, an interracial group of fifteen men strongly committed to nonviolent direct action boarded Greyhound and

Jim Crow

Jim Crow laws are named after "Jim Crow," an African American character ridiculed in minstrel shows in the 1800s. Minstrel actors were white, but painted their faces black and sang and danced in a way that made fun of African Americans, especially their speaking patterns. White people who believed that they were superior to black people instituted Jim Crow laws and social practices to exert power over African Americans, beginning shortly after the Civil War. It was legalized racism.

Library of Congress

The laws and customs required segregation in cemeteries, prisons, libraries, buses, and trains. There were separate schools, churches, hospitals, waiting rooms, drinking fountains, and public bathrooms. Facilities for black people were often grossly inferior to facilities for white people. Interracial marriage was illegal and the right of African Americans to vote was also effectively eliminated by Jim Crow laws.

African Americans were to act submissively to white people and any sort of interaction between a black man and a white woman, including touching, speaking, or even looking was forbidden. Breaking any of the Jim Crow laws could result in arrest, or worse. The threat of lynching—brutal murder by a crowd, often by hanging—was used to enforce Jim Crow laws, both written and unwritten.

Trailways buses. It was a tense day for the activists. They knew all too well that Thurgood Marshall might be right—that their actions might provoke local thugs to beat or even murder them. Frightened, but determined to remain nonviolent, the riders climbed aboard their buses in Washington, DC, and left for Richmond, Virginia.

The first leg of the trip saw no incidents of violence. The activists sat, racially mixed, in both the front and back of the buses, while others sat alone as observers, prepared to educate drivers and passengers about the Supreme Court decision and to help defuse any tensions that might erupt.

Trouble began to brew in North Carolina. Bayard was threatened with arrest in Blackstone and Oxford, but neither threat resulted in

The Journey of Reconciliation–Standing outside office of Attorney S.W. Robinson in Richmond, Virginia. Members included (left to right): Worth Randle, Wallace Nelson, Ernest Bromley, James Peck, Igal Roodenko, Bayard Rustin, Joe Felmet, George Houser and Andrew Johnson.

jail. In another bus, on the way to Raleigh, African American rider Conrad Lynn was arrested and thrown in jail. In Durham, Bayard and two others were arrested, but they were released without being charged.

When the group arrived in Chapel Hill, they were met by Reverend Charles Jones, a local white Presbyterian minister and FOR member. The riders led public discussions in town about the *Morgan* decision, nonviolent direct action, and racial justice. The talks were well received. The next morning, April 13, as the group was getting ready to leave Chapel Hill for Greensboro, North Carolina, local white segregationists began to respond.

Joe Felmet and Andrew Johnson—an interracial pair sitting in the front of a Greyhound—were arrested before the bus departed. Felmet, who was white, was physically thrown off the bus. On the same bus, Bayard and white rider Igal Roodenko took the place of Felmet and Johnson, and they too were promptly arrested. White

Bayard Rustin and George Houser wrote this song about their experiences with the Journey of Reconciliation.

You don't have to ride Jim Crow,
No, you don't have to ride Jim Crow.
On June the third, the High Court said
When you ride interstate, Jim Crow is dead.
You don't have to ride Jim Crow.

And when you get on the bus
And when you get on the bus
Get on the bus, sit anyplace
'Cause Irene Morgan won her case.
You don't have to ride Jim Crow.

Now you can set anywhere
Now you can set anywhere
Set anywhere, don't raise no fuss.
Keep cool brother, your cause is just.
You don't have to ride Jim Crow.

And if that driver man says "move"
And if that driver man says "move"
If driver say "move" speak up polite
But sit there tight, you're in the right.
You don't have to ride Jim Crow.

You don't have to ride Jim Crow,
No, you don't have to ride Jim Crow.
Go quiet-like and face arrest.
NAACP will make that test.
You don't have to ride Jim Crow.

And someday we'll all be free.
Yes, someday we'll all be free.
When united action turns the tide
And black and white sit side by side.
Oh, someday we'll all be free.

rider James Peck then went to the police station to check on his arrested friends. By then, a crowd of white taxi drivers had gathered from the nearby taxi stand. When Peck tried to reboard the bus, one of the drivers delivered a fierce blow to his head, complaining that Peck had come down South just to "stir up the n*****s."[48] Peck began to bleed and collapsed from the attack.

When Jones learned about the bloody incident, he rushed to the police station. He helped arrange for bail and took the group of riders back to his home. A gang of taxi drivers followed them in two cabs, pulled up in front of the house, and got out of the cabs armed with sticks and rocks.

Mrs. Jones began to receive phone calls warning her and her family that the riders would be lynched and her house burned down. She fled with her two children as a mob began to surround the house. Terrified, but still committed to nonviolence, the riders huddled together and planned their next moves as stones came crashing through the first-floor windows.

Eventually, white police officers arrived, and although they did not arrest the mob, they held the crowd back to allow a line of cars to take the frightened riders safely to Greensboro.

There were additional arrests, but nothing came close to the life-threatening incident in Chapel Hill. Bayard and the other riders were relieved as they pulled into Washington, DC on April 22 and 23 and headed home.

The historic Journey of Reconciliation called attention to the continuing practice of illegally segregating interstate bus passengers. With the help of African American journalists accompanying them, the riders publicized the *Morgan* decision across the four Southern states and beyond. By informing so many people of the Supreme Court ruling, and by their steadfast courage in the face of violence, these "first freedom riders," as they came to be called, inspired others to take their own stand against racial injustice.

Eight years later, Rosa Parks refused to surrender her seat to a white passenger on a segregated bus in Montgomery, Alabama. Fourteen years later, interracial groups of men and women embarked on similar journeys, dubbed "The Freedom Rides," throughout the Deep South, where they were beaten, arrested, and jailed, attracting national media attention and the outrage of politicians and ordinary citizens devoted to civil rights. The men who took part in the Journey of Reconciliation helped to spur a new wave of activism that would eventually lead the nation to demand that the South abide by the Supreme Court decision in *Morgan* and eliminate racial segregation in transportation.

Bayard picketed the French consulate and embassy in 1950 to protest the arrest of Garry Davis, a former U.S. bomber pilot and founder of a world citizenship movement. The French authorities had arrested Davis after he had staged a public protest of the government's decision to imprison a conscientious objector.

chapter 10

JIM CROW ARMY

Although the Journey of Reconciliation was behind them, some riders still faced trials in the cities where they were arrested. In Chapel Hill, North Carolina, Andrew Johnson, Joe Felmet, Igal Roodenko, and Bayard Rustin were found guilty of violating North Carolina's bus seating statute. Johnson had to pay a fine, while the others were sentenced to a chain gang.

The four arrested in Chapel Hill were the only riders to be convicted. All the others either had charges dropped or their cases were thrown out of court. Bayard and the others did not expect that they would have to serve their sentences, since NAACP lawyers were helping them appeal their sentences to higher courts. The appeals process could take years, but Bayard did not sit idly by while the lawyers appealed the case. He had work to do.

Bayard continued to protest racial discrimination whenever and wherever he could—by sitting in the *whites only* section of a train's dining car, for example—but events in Washington were now drawing his attention. World War II was over, but President Harry S. Truman and Congress wanted to continue to draft men to serve in the military, which remained segregated. This was offensive to Bayard's Quaker beliefs in pacifism and equality because it promoted both war and inequality.

A. Philip Randolph (right) founded the Committee to End Jim Crow in the Military to fight segregation. He and Grant Reynolds are shown here, testifying before the Senate Armed Services Committee in 1948.

Bayard joined with George Houser, his colleague from the Journey of Reconciliation, and A. Philip Randolph of the March on Washington Movement to work toward preventing a peacetime draft and ending segregation in the military. Randolph and other African American leaders met with the president in March 1948. Randolph told him, "Negroes . . . resent the idea of fighting or being drafted into another Jim Crow army."[51] Bayard, Randolph, and others picketed the White House with signs that said things like *If we must die for our country let us die as free men—not as Jim Crow slaves.* Randolph delivered a speech calling for "Negroes and freedom-loving whites in the armed forces . . . to consider laying down their guns in protest."[52]

Despite the pickets and speeches, on June 24, 1948, President Truman signed a new peacetime draft law that preserved racial segregation in the military.

Bayard and Houser were outraged. They organized picket lines and held street rallies encouraging young men to go to jail rather than serve in the military. Meanwhile, Randolph declared that he was fully prepared to "oppose a Jim Crow Army until I rot in jail."[53]

On July 26, 1948, just as the campaign was gaining steam, President Truman issued an executive order declaring "there shall be equality of treatment and opportunity for all persons in the armed services without regard to race, color, religion, or national origin. This policy shall be put into effect as rapidly as possible."[54]

Bayard was skeptical. Just as *Morgan v. Virginia* had not automatically ended segregation on buses, the president's executive order did not prevent military leaders from continuing racial segregation. But Randolph was pleased with Truman's change of mind and ended his plan for civil disobedience. Angry at Randolph's decision, Bayard issued a public statement criticizing Randolph for giving up the fight. He organized picket lines and a street rally in New York, where over 300 people protested the draft and segregation. He and his friend Jim Peck were promptly arrested for disorderly conduct. While serving a fifteen-day sentence in jail, Bayard suffered intense criticism from Randolph and realized that his campaign against segregation was not working, so he allowed it to fizzle out. It was a tough battle to lose. The disagreement with Randolph had caused damage to their relationship that took over a year to heal. And Bayard had been right—it would be years before the military was actually desegregated.

Disappointed with his own country, he turned his attention to world events. On October 1, 1948, just days after his release from jail, Bayard boarded the *Queen Mary* and sailed across the Atlantic to Great Britain and France, and then on to India for a seven-week tour. He was accompanied to India by renowned British pacifist Muriel Lester, a leader in the international FOR. Under Mohandas Gandhi's leadership, Indians had waged a successful nonviolent revolution, winning independence from Great Britain in 1947. But not long after that victory, Gandhi was assassinated, shot by a Hindu who believed he was too tolerant of other religions.

Bayard had been invited to India by nonviolent leaders, including Mohandas Gandhi's son, Devadas, but he was disappointed to find that interest in nonviolence and pacifism there was fading. India's new political leaders were intent on building a huge military,

British pacifist Muriel Lester was struck by Bayard's unique abilities to connect with audiences filled with people of color. "He can do, and does at once, three times as much as a white pacifist," she wrote.[55]

Bayard met with Indian Prime Minister Jawaharlal Nehru.

beginning their own military draft, and commanding respect as a regional and world power, almost mimicking the behavior of their former British rulers. Such a vision contradicted Gandhi's firm, but humble, approach to wielding political power.

Bayard found himself in the strange and sometimes uncomfortable position of explaining the continuing relevance of nonviolence to Gandhi's onetime followers.

Bayard captivated his audiences with stories about how he used Gandhi's methods to fight racial injustice in the United States. Part of his warm reception was also due to Bayard's willingness to "go native"— to eat Indian food, dress in the style of homespun clothes worn by Gandhi's followers, and use the familiar Indian greeting. Rather than shaking his guests' hands, Bayard held his palms together in front of his chest, his fingers pointing upward. Bowing slightly, he said, "Na-mas-te," meaning "I bow to the divine in you," a reverential greeting commonly used by Hindus and others in India.

Bayard enjoyed his time in India, making sure to keep company not only with powerful politicians, like Prime Minister Nehru, but also with "untouchables," people deemed to be impure and not worthy of rights enjoyed by other Indians. The trip was a resounding success, and left Bayard with a renewed sense of the power of nonviolence and a strong desire to bring Gandhi's tactics of mass action to the fight for social justice in the United States.

He departed for home, his enthusiasm dampened by what he knew waited for him there. The North Carolina Supreme Court had finally made a decision about his arrest during the Journey of Reconciliation. Bayard was bound for the chain gang.

This photo of a Southern chain gang was taken between 1900 and 1906.

11

CHAINS

Once again, Bayard was off to jail. At the end of March 1949 he began serving a 30-day sentence imposed by the court for his arrest in North Carolina during the 1947 Journey of Reconciliation. The riders had appealed their guilty verdicts, but the Superior Court judge had ruled that the US Supreme Court decision in *Morgan v. Virginia* did not apply to Bayard, because on the day of his arrest, he was an *intra*state passenger (traveling within the state), not an *inter*state passenger (traveling between states); his departure and destination points, Chapel Hill and Greensboro, were both in North Carolina.

Bayard and his fellow riders appealed the sentence to the state's Supreme Court. The final appeal was denied; Bayard would have to serve his sentence. He had been in jail many times before but had never served on a chain gang. He told a newspaper reporter, "We understand that while the work is hard, the conditions are not too terrible." Such a notion proved to be quite wrong.[56]

Bayard served his sentence at Roxboro, a prison camp for African Americans in North Carolina. Overrun with cockroaches, the living quarters with their mud-covered floors were overcrowded and foul-smelling. Bayard reported that he did not get a single full night's sleep while there. Working conditions were just as bad. Chained

A typical day at Roxboro Prison Camp[59]

5:30–7:00	Wake-up bell
	Make bed
	Wash Face
	Breakfast: Oatmeal with no sugar or milk, fried baloney, stewed apples, coffee
7:00–12:00	Work hard for five hours with one fifteen-minute smoking break
12:00–12:30	Lunch: beans, fatty bacon, molasses, cornbread
12:30–5:30	Work hard for five hours with one fifteen-minute smoking break
5:30–6:30	Supper: Cabbage and boiled potatoes OR macaroni and stewed tomatoes
	Supper on Sundays: Corned beef, vegetables, and apple cobbler
6:30–8:30	Locked in the dormitory
8:30–5:30	Sleep

together with other prisoners, Bayard served on the road crew, smashing rocks and digging trenches under the hot sun ten hours a day. A heavily armed guard made it virtually impossible to escape into the surrounding woods.

The guards brutalized and terrorized prisoners. Sometimes they made prisoners "dance" by shooting at their feet. They used clubs, leather straps, or their steel-toed boots to beat and kick the prisoners. One chain-ganger Bayard met spent two weeks in solitary confinement with just three crackers a day to eat. The guards even chained prisoners' arms to the bars of their cells, leaving them to dangle in midair for hours, or even days. It was torture, plain and simple.

This kind of treatment made most of the prisoners angry and resentful of the guards. Relying on his Quaker beliefs in human dignity and his training in nonviolence, Bayard decided to try something different. "I would try to work more willingly and harder than

Chain Gang Songs

Little did Bayard know in 1940, when he recorded the album *Chain Gang* with Josh White and his Carolinians, that one day he would serve time on an actual chain gang.

Got a nine foot shovel, my pick is four foot long.
Got a nine foot shovel, my pick is four foot long.
I'm in the world of trouble when I'm singin' this song.

If you use a pick and shovel, sure cain't mess around.
If you ain't a man, sure God bring you down.
'Cos I've been shovellin' (shovellin') all day just like a fool.
I'll tell you, buddy, they don't teach that in school.
　　　　　　　　　　– from "Nine Foot Shovel" on *Chain Gang*

Well, I always been in trouble, 'cause I'm a black-skinned man.
Said I hit a white man, [and they] locked me in the can.
They took me to the stockade, wouldn't give me no trial.
The judge said, "You black boy, forty years on the hard rock pile."
　　　　　　　　　　　　　　　– from "Trouble" on *Chain Gang*

Just as sure as the train, boys, rolls up in the yard.
I'm gonna leave this rock pile if I have to ride the rods.
I'm goin home, boys, cry'n won't make me stay.
My time is up, throw these chains away.
　　　　　　　　　　– from "Goin' Home Boys" on *Chain Gang*

Chains 'round my shoulder, my feet is bracelet bound.
Jump when cap'n calls you, or else he'll knock you down.
I hear danger singin', I hear danger moan.
Cryin' who? Cryin' you!

Sleep on a pallet in a dirty cell.
Sure could sleep better if I was dead in hell.
I hear danger singin', I hear danger moan.
Cryin' who? Cryin' you!
　　　　　　　– from "Cryin' Who? Cryin' You!" on *Chain Gang*

anyone in the crew, and I would be as polite and considerate as possible."[57] His efforts paid off. Bayard and "Captain Jones" (the man who supervised the work crew) "came to recognize that despite our different attitudes we could work together and learn from each other."[58] Shortly before his release, Bayard even sent Jones a letter expressing pleasure at working on his crew, thanking him for soda and other treats, and wishing him well in his recovery from a cold.

Bayard viewed chain gangs as cruel and unusual punishment, something prohibited under the US Constitution. Furthermore, they were a grave injustice to human dignity and the spirit of prisoners. He could not remain silent, so after returning to New York, Bayard published an article, "Twenty-Two Days on a Chain Gang," in two major newspapers—*The New York Post* and *The Afro-American*. The article depicted the brutality of chain gangs so effectively that it meant the end of chain gangs in North Carolina. Bayard's efforts placed him squarely in the rich tradition of Quakers who had long fought against prisoner abuse and for a more humane system that focused on rehabilitation rather than on punishment or revenge.

A REPORT ON

TWENTY-TWO DAYS ON THE CHAIN GANG

AT ROXBORO, NORTH CAROLINA

by

Bayard Rustin

PLEASE NOTE CAREFULLY

(1) The information in this report is con-
fidential. Under no circumstances should
any part of it be repeated or published.
There are two reasons for this decision.

a. Liberal North Carolinians should
decide how this material can best be
used to better conditions

b. No publicity should be given until
this report has reached the proper state
authorities.

(2) The material in this report is tentative
and is being sent to you for your recom-
mendations and suggestions. Will you give
us the benefit of your experience and make
any corrections, suggestions, or additions
that you feel will improve or make this
report more useful.

The cover of Bayard's report recounting the brutal conditions of a North Carolina chain gang. Written for the Fellowship of Reconciliation (FOR) it was later serialized in The New York Post newspaper.

Picketing against nuclear weapons in 1950.

chapter 12

A REPUTATION IN THE FIELD

Back home in New York, Bayard continued speaking out about the dangers of atomic weapons, as he had since 1945, when US bombs caused so much destruction in Japan. The threat of nuclear war loomed even larger in 1950, not only because of the proliferation of nuclear weapons, but also because of increasing tensions created by the Cold War between the US and the Soviet Union.

The Cold War made it difficult for Bayard to spread the message of peace and nonviolence. Many people were terrified that the Soviet Union would conquer the United States and destroy the American way of life. Bayard found US citizens "so fearful and demoralized" that they failed to question, let alone resist, the government's policy of building more nuclear bombs to aim at the Soviet Union.[60]

Bayard believed that letters, telegrams, and speeches were not enough. A direct action campaign was also necessary. He proposed lying on the ground in front of facilities that built nuclear weapons to prevent delivery of the materials they needed. While he thought the entire staff of the FOR should get arrested, the FOR leadership did not agree.

Bayard and other radical pacifists refused to eat during a week-long "fast for peace" in Washington, DC. The protesters also held silent vigils inside the Pentagon and outside the Soviet Embassy,

The Cold War

The United States and the Soviet Union were no longer allies, as they had been in World War II. The two superpowers were now involved in an intense rivalry, each seeking to dominate the other with the strongest economy, political system, and military in the world. Marked by hostility just short of violent conflict, this rivalry became known as the Cold War.

To make matters worse, by 1949, both the US and Soviet Union had nuclear weapons. If the Cold War ever got "hot" and one country used its nuclear weapons, the other was sure to retaliate, which would be a worldwide disaster.

As communism spread, tensions built. After World War II, several countries in Eastern Europe came under communist control. In 1949, China became a communist country. The Korean peninsula, formerly controlled by Japan, was cut in half and North Korea became a communist country, friendly to the Soviet Union and China. South Korea was a capitalist country allied with the United States. In 1950, North Korea invaded South Korea, triggering the Korean War. The US entered the war, fighting on the South Korean side.

McCarthyism

The Cold War fed on people's fear of communism in other countries. But this era also saw increased suspicion of Americans. Senator Joseph McCarthy and others claimed that the US government was infiltrated with communists. These claims were often unfounded, but the accused were made to testify before Congress about their own associations with communists. They were also encouraged to name other potential communists.

The accusation alone could get a person fired, or even blacklisted. Blacklisted people, often in the entertainment industry, were prevented from working anywhere in their field. Two of Bayard's colleagues from his Broadway performance in *John Henry*, Paul Robeson and Josh White, were blacklisted.

Apartheid

Apartheid (an Afrikaans word translated as "apartness") referred to a system of racial segregation established in 1948 by South Africa's white political leaders. Like the Jim Crow laws of the southern United States, apartheid was used to intimidate and control the non-white population. Native black South Africans, so-called "coloureds" (people of mixed race), and Indian immigrants were segregated from white South Africans in neighborhoods, transportation, schools, and other public places. Apartheid also imposed curfews and travel restrictions.

affirming that both "superpowers" should be held accountable for the nuclear threat. They also protested against US involvement in the Korean War.

The campaigns in the US to stop nuclear proliferation and end the Korean War were unsuccessful, so, once again, Bayard turned his attention to other parts of the world.

In South Africa, the African National Congress, a political party dedicated to gaining equal rights for black South Africans, organized nonviolent protest rallies. Gandhi had also fought discrimination by nonviolent direct action in South Africa from 1893 to 1914. Bayard and George Houser began to devise ways to assist the Gandhian campaign in South Africa.

In August 1952, Bayard visited Africa's Gold Coast and Nigeria, both still British colonies. Black leaders there were building a political movement to win independence from Great Britain. Once home, Bayard told A.J. Muste that he wanted to return to West Africa to establish a center for training in the philosophy and tactics of nonviolence. Bayard was convinced that nonviolent methods could work in the struggle for liberation. He was also sure he was the right pacifist to operate the center. As he put it, "a Negro with a reputation in the field of nonviolent work—certainly not a white person—is needed for success."[61]

After considerable debate, the FOR leadership approved Bayard's return to West Africa for a full year. Bayard was elated and he began a speaking tour to heighten awareness of Africa and to raise funds for his trip. But the excitement would soon end.

The US government continued to test nuclear weapons.

chapter 13

BAYARD'S PROBLEM

In January of 1953, Bayard found himself in a jail in California. He had been in jail before, of course, for protesting against war and segregation, but now it was different. This time the charge was "lewd vagrancy."[62]

He had been in Pasadena to give an evening lecture on world peace sponsored by the American Friends Service Committee. Late that night, he was arrested for homosexual behavior, which was against the law.

Although Bayard had not hidden his sexual orientation from his friends or coworkers, he had been careful not to make it a public matter. That night he had been careless. Now that it was in his police record, and in the newspaper, it became very public.

Back in New York, A.J. Muste was furious. He had known about Bayard's sexual orientation for years, and he saw it as a threat to Bayard's work with the FOR. He wanted Bayard to "give up" homosexuality and had encouraged him to get treatment for what many believed was a mental illness. He had also warned Bayard that if he did not control his sexual behavior, he would have to resign from the FOR. The arrest was, to Muste, a betrayal.

The FOR quickly announced, "To our great sorrow Bayard Rustin was convicted on a 'morals charge' (homosexual) and sentenced to 60 days in the Los Angeles County Jail on January 23, 1953. As of

Witch Hunts

Communists were not the only targets of the McCarthy era. Homosexuals were persecuted, as well. Gossip and rumors flew as thousands of homosexuals (and heterosexuals merely suspected of being gay) lost their jobs during this time.

A few months after Bayard's arrest in Pasadena, President Eisenhower issued an executive order excluding certain people from federal jobs: "Any criminal, infamous, dishonest, immoral, or notoriously disgraceful conduct, habitual use of intoxicants to excess, drug addiction, or sexual perversion."[66] This included homosexuals.

Franklin D. Roosevelt's executive order in 1941 had desegregated the defense industry. Harry S. Truman's executive order in 1948 had desegregated the military. These executive orders worked toward an end to discrimination. In contrast, Dwight D. Eisenhower's executive order in 1953 *required* the government to discriminate against gays and lesbians.

that date, and at his own suggestion, his service as an FOR staff member terminated."[63]

It was not just Muste's personal disapproval of Bayard's actions that mattered. Other FOR members also turned their backs on Bayard because of his arrest. They believed that public knowledge of Bayard's "problem" damaged the FOR's reputation and jeopardized its efforts to promote peace.[64] With twelve years of work with the FOR at an end, Bayard sank into depression.

After his release from prison, Bayard returned to New York, where a psychiatrist helped him regain his confidence and think about the future. After six months, friends helped him get a job developing peace programs for the War Resisters League (WRL), a secular pacifist organization based in New York City.

In 1954, Bayard reconnected with some of his Quaker colleagues in the AFSC when they invited him to participate in a group working on a seventy-page booklet about Quaker pacifism in relation to the Cold War and other world conflicts. Bayard was perfect for the job.

Bayard enjoyed working with the group on the writing project, but several AFSC members were concerned about his 1953 arrest in Pasadena. After considerable debate and personal soul searching,

> "It has been truly said that as our strength approaches infinity, our security approaches zero. The H-bomb gives us, not the power to secure ourselves, but only the power to destroy the world."
>
> — *Speak Truth to Power*[67]
>
> "[Nonviolence] relies upon love rather than hate, and though it involves a willingness to accept rather than inflict suffering, it is neither passive nor cowardly."
>
> — *Speak Truth to Power*[68]

Bayard conceded that the appearance of his name might detract from the importance of the document's message of nonviolence. In a letter to Steve Cary, chairman of the writing group, he said, "I feel that my being listed might very well lead to some new attack which might gravely delay the time when I can again be useful."[65]

Speak Truth to Power: A Quaker Search for an Alternative to Violence was published in 1955 and became an important source of information and inspiration for peace workers. The phrase "speak truth to power" (which some claim was first used by Bayard) became a popular slogan for Quakers and other activists. Bayard and Muste contributed major ideas that went into the project. Muste was listed as one of the thirteen authors. Bayard was not.

By then, Bayard was organizing another nonviolent protest.

"Operation Alert" was like a fire drill for nuclear war. Every year between 1954 and 1961, the US Civil Defense Administration conducted a simulated nuclear attack on several major US cities. People were required by law to evacuate public places and open spaces and go to "safe" locations in preparation for a nuclear strike. Bayard and other peace activists believed it was wrong to cooperate with any preparations for nuclear war. Furthermore, it was misleading and silly to pretend that one could be safe from a nuclear blast by walking into a building. The destruction wrought upon Hiroshima and Nagasaki proved that.

On June 15, 1955, sirens blared in New York City. People rushed for imaginary shelter from the imaginary nuclear bombs. But Bayard and other activists did not seek shelter. They sat quietly on benches in City Hall Park, where they were arrested.

Bayard with Martin Luther King, Jr. in 1956. Bayard and King got along well and engaged in numerous conversations about different strategies of nonviolence—boycotts, marches, rallies, sit-ins, strikes, and more—and about pacifism as a way of life.

chapter 14
THE MONTGOMERY IMPROVEMENT ASSOCIATION

On the buses in Montgomery, Alabama, African American passengers were required to give up their seats to white passengers. In 1955, some refused and were arrested. Rosa Parks was probably the best known of these, but she was not the first.

Claudette Colvin, a 15-year-old student at Booker T. Washington High School, refused in March.

Aurelia Browder, a 34-year-old widow, refused in April.

18-year-old Mary Louise Smith refused in October.

Rosa Parks, a 42-year-old seamstress, refused on December 1. She was an active member of the local NAACP and it was her arrest that ignited a major boycott of the city's buses by African American riders. Rather than ride on segregated buses, Montgomery's black residents walked or carpooled.

The Montgomery bus boycott has become the symbolic beginning of the modern civil rights movement and marked the rise of Reverend Martin Luther King, Jr. King had recently arrived in Montgomery and was the pastor of Dexter Avenue Baptist Church. Though he was only 26 years old, he was elected to be the president of a new organization, the Montgomery Improvement Association (MIA). In his new role, King became the leading spokesman for African Americans in Montgomery, who demanded that seating on

White Citizens' Councils

On May 17, 1954, the United States Supreme Court ruled in *Brown v. Board of Education* that the idea of "separate but equal" education was wrong, and that segregation of public schools was unconstitutional.

In response to the *Brown v. Board* decision, white people in the South joined together to form White Citizens' Councils. Unlike the secretive Ku Klux Klan, the White Citizens' Councils operated in public. They opposed integration of schools and worked to deny the civil rights of African Americans.

The actions of the White Citizens' Councils resulted in African Americans being evicted from their rental properties, denied loans, and fired from their jobs. The Councils also used intimidation, threats, and violence.

buses be on a first-come, first-served basis, that drivers be more courteous to black passengers, and that the bus company assign black drivers to routes that served mostly African Americans.

As an activist devoted to racial justice, Bayard was captivated by the drama unfolding in Montgomery. The situation there had become very tense. The White Citizens' Council (WCC) used threats and violence against the boycotters, and distributed thousands of fliers claiming: "We hold these truths to be self-evident: that all whites are created equal with certain rights; among these are life, liberty and the pursuit of dead n*****s."[69] Members of the WCC bombed the homes of King and E.D. Nixon, a leader in the local NAACP and an active member of Randolph's union, The Brotherhood of Sleeping Car Porters.

In the face of such violence, Bayard worried that the boycotters would fight back, and he believed that any violent response on the part of African Americans would be used to justify even more violence against them. So, under the guidance of Randolph, he and his colleagues at the WRL agreed that Bayard should travel to Montgomery to try to convince the leadership to remain nonviolent. Despite the risks, he was eager to go and planned to lead workshops on the philosophy and tactics of Gandhian nonviolence.

Bayard wrote this song for the Montgomery Improvement Association (sung to the tune of *Give Me That Old Time Religion*).

We are moving on to vict'ry (3x)
With hope and dignity.

We shall all stand together (3x)
Till everyone is free.

We know love is the watchword (3x)
For peace and liberty.

Black and white, all are brothers (3x)
To live in harmony.

We are moving on to vict'ry (3x)
With hope and dignity.

Before he left for Montgomery, Bayard learned that African American ministers and train workers had been smuggling guns into the hands of local activists. When he arrived in Montgomery on February 21, he discovered first-hand that the racial situation was "like war."[70] As he walked around the African American neighborhoods, he spotted armed guards protecting the homes of the movement's leaders, including King, E.D. Nixon, and Reverend Ralph David Abernathy (King's best friend and right-hand man). Fearing another bombing, supporters had strung lights outside King's house and posted armed bodyguards there around the clock.

King was out of town that day, but Bayard introduced himself to Nixon and Abernathy. They invited Bayard to come to strategy sessions, and he happily accepted. Although he had come to Montgomery to run workshops on nonviolence, Bayard soon found himself undertaking a wide variety of tasks. One of the first things he did was to write lyrics for a song emphasizing protest, unity, nonviolence, and equality. MIA leaders used the song at mass meetings to inspire and instruct the boycotters. Bayard also helped organize car pools and write publicity material and press releases about the boycott.

Perhaps most important, Bayard began making concrete suggestions about acting in a Gandhian manner, with dignity and

Pilgrimage to Nonviolence

In *Stride Toward Freedom*, King's book about the Montgomery boycott, he described the aspects of nonviolence used in the boycott.

• It is not passive nonresistance to evil, it is active nonviolent resistance to evil.

• ... it does not seek to defeat or humiliate the opponent, but to win his friendship and understanding.

• ... [it] is directed against forces of evil rather than against persons who happen to be doing the evil.

• The nonviolent resister is willing to accept violence if necessary, but never to inflict it.

• The nonviolent resister not only refuses to shoot his opponent but he also refuses to hate him.

• ... it is based on the conviction that the universe is on the side of justice.[74]

nonviolence. On the day he arrived, a jury formally charged 115 boycott leaders with breaking Alabama's law against organizing boycotts. Bayard suggested to the leaders that rather than allowing the sheriff to seek them out like common criminals, they should put on their best clothes, march in dignified fashion to the courthouse, and surrender themselves to the legal authorities. The leaders followed Bayard's advice, and as they walked up the court steps, hundreds of supporters clapped and cheered. As Bayard described it, "White community leaders, politicians, and police were flabbergasted. Negroes were thrilled to see their leaders surrender without being hunted down."[71] The event energized the boycotters and made them proud of themselves and their campaign.

The boycotters were enthusiastic, but they were not always sure about which tactics to use in their fight against segregation. Even King, who had studied Gandhi, did not know much about the strategies and tactics of nonviolence. In fact, King was not a pacifist at that time. For example, after his house was bombed, he applied for a gun permit. Although the state of Alabama denied his request, guns were a common sight inside King's home.

Still, King was open to learning more about nonviolence, and Bayard was eager to teach him. With Bayard's help, King came to understand that pacifists strive to be nonviolent in attitude and action at all times. They believe that every person possesses dignity and has a right to life.

Bayard also helped King understand how important it was for the boycott leader to be nonviolent at all times, not just when nonviolence seemed to work. "If . . . a leader's house is bombed, and he shoots back," Bayard told King, "then that is an encouragement to his followers to pick up guns."[72]

Convinced by Bayard and other pacifists, King began to embrace pacifism as a way of life, not just as a useful tactic for fighting segregation on buses. As the boycott continued, he removed the guns from his house, instructed the bodyguards to patrol without carrying weapons, and encouraged all boycotters to become nonviolent in attitude and action. The boycott became known across the world as a peaceful protest, and King developed a reputation as a nonviolent leader.

Meanwhile, members of the White Citizens' Council, including local police officers, grew suspicious of this outsider from New York City and began watching Bayard closely and using wiretaps to listen to his private telephone conversations. "I have been followed by police cars and never go out after dark alone," he wrote in a letter. He also learned that a local news reporter was spreading a rumor that he was "a communist NAACP organizer . . . planning a violent uprising."[73] This was false, of course; Bayard was doing everything he could to keep a violent uprising from happening.

Bayard also worried that the WCC would learn about his 1953 arrest in California and publicize that information to tarnish the boycott's reputation. He talked with King about his concerns and they agreed it would be best for Bayard to leave Montgomery, while continuing to advise the boycott leadership from afar.

Back in New York, Bayard stayed in close contact with King by mail and phone. He helped raise thousands of dollars for the boycott; wrote speeches for King; introduced King to important activists, including Randolph and Muste; publicized news about the boycott across the country; organized a huge New York City rally for King and the boycott; wrote an article about Montgomery,

Browder v. Gayle

King worked with the NAACP to file a federal lawsuit (*Browder v. Gayle*) on February 1, 1956, in US District Court. The case claimed that Alabama's bus segregation laws were unconstitutional. The plaintiffs in the case—Aurelia Browder, Susie McDonald, Claudette Colvin, and Mary Louise Smith—had all been mistreated on Montgomery buses because of their race. The defendant, W.A. Gayle, was the mayor of Montgomery and a member of the Montgomery White Citizens' Council.

On June 13, 1956, the District Court ruled that racial segregation on buses was unconstitutional and ordered the buses to be desegregated.

But the battle was not won yet. The city of Montgomery and the state of Alabama took the case to the US Supreme Court.

the first that was published under King's name; and planned non-violence workshops for people new to the movement.

All their hard work paid off, as did the lawsuit filed by the NAACP. On November 13, 1956, the US Supreme Court ruled in *Browder v. Gayle* that Alabama's bus segregation laws were unconstitutional. The sweeping decision meant that the entire state of Alabama would have to allow black passengers to sit wherever they wanted on buses traveling within the state. No longer would bus passengers see signs directing "colored" riders to the back of the bus. Never again would Rosa Parks have to surrender her seat to a white rider. The Montgomery boycotters and their supporters across the country had won a victory that exceeded their original demands.

On December 21, 1956, King boarded one of Montgomery's newly integrated buses, selecting a seat right near the front. He did not gloat, smirk, or act arrogantly. He rode with dignity, making sure not to provoke any violent actions against African American riders, just as he and Bayard had discussed.

But Bayard did not ride with King.

Bayard thought that his presence there might reignite false charges that he was an outside agitator, a communist, and a criminal.

So while his heart was with all the African American riders as they rode integrated buses, Bayard remained far away, back in New York, where he was planning his next steps on the road to freedom.

SOUTHERN NEGRO LEADERS CONFERENCE ON TRANSPORTATION AND NON-VIOLENT INTEGRATION

Ebenezer Baptist Church
407 Auburn Avenue
Atlanta, Georgia

WORKING PAPERS for Founding of SCLC.

January 10 - 11, 1957
:-:-:-:-:-:-:-:-:-:-:-:-:-

W O R K I N G   P A P E R   # 1

THE MEANING OF THE BUS PROTEST
in the
SOUTHERN STRUGGLE FOR TOTAL INTEGRATION

In analyzing the Bus Protest certain factors emerge:

1. These protests are directly related to economic survival, since the masses of people use busses to reach their work. The people are therefore interested in what happens in busses.

2. The people know that in bus segregation they have a just grievance. No one had to arouse their social anger.

3. In refusing to ride the busses the people pledge a daily rededication. This daily act becomes a matter of group pride.

4. Unlike many problems, such as integrated education, there is no administrative machinery and legal maneuvering that stand between the people and the act of staying off the busses, or sitting in front seats. The situation permits direct action.

5. The campaign is based on the most stable social institution in Negro culture - the church.

6. The protest requires community sharing through mass meetings, contributions, economic assistance, hitchhiking etc.

7. The situation permits and requires a unified leadership.

8. The method of non-violence - Christian love, makes humble folk noble and turns fear into courage.

9. The exigencies of the struggle create a community spirit through community sacrifice.

N O T E :
The underlined words are 9 qualities required for mass movement. When a group of people have developed them in one area, these qualities can be transferred to any other constructive one through education by action, the final quality.

The first of 7 "working papers" documenting the factors that made the boycott so successful and leading to the founding of the Southern Christian Leadership Conference (SCLS), Dr. King's organizational base.

A flyer urging people to join the 1957 Prayer Pilgrimage for Freedom. Held at the Lincoln Memorial in Washington, it was the occasion for Dr. King's first national address.

FROM THE COURTS TO COMMUNITY ACTION

The NAACP had scored three land-mark Supreme Court victories. Segregation had been ruled unconstitutional on interstate buses (*Morgan v. Virginia*, 1946), in public schools (*Brown v. Board of Education*, 1954), and on city buses (*Browder v. Gayle*, 1956). But each case took a long time to reach the Supreme Court. Instead of waiting for the court to affirm their constitutional rights, Bayard thought that African American people should become personally engaged in a public and dramatic struggle for their freedom.

> "We conclude that, in the field of public education, the doctrine of 'separate but equal' has no place. Separate educational facilities are inherently unequal."
>
> — *Brown v. Board of Education*, 347 US 483

Court decisions advancing civil rights did not mean a thing if political leaders simply ignored or resisted the court orders. Bayard believed that "the center of gravity" in the civil rights movement had "shifted from the courts to community action." Nonviolent tactics like marches, rallies, picketing, "sit-ins," and boycotts had helped Gandhi win independence for India. Bayard saw these same techniques as the way to turn court decisions into reality. "We must recognize in this new period," he wrote, *that direct action is our most potent political weapon.*[75]

Speakers at the Prayer Pilgrimage for Freedom included (left to right): Roy Wilkins, A. Philip Randolph, Thomas Kilgore, Jr., and Martin Luther King, Jr.

Bayard went to King with an idea.

Throughout the boycott, Bayard had been a close advisor to King, even when he was far from Alabama. Although King was a brilliant visionary and a masterful speaker, Bayard once said that King "did not have the ability to organize vampires to go to a bloodbath."[76] Thus, it was often Bayard's job to draw up the concrete plans to bring King's visions to life.

With King's approval, Bayard and his colleagues developed plans for something radically different from the NAACP. This new organization would eventually be named the Southern Christian Leadership Conference (SCLC). While the NAACP had been successful in the courts, the SCLC would use nonviolent direct action to secure civil rights for African Americans throughout the South.

King brought together sixty prominent southern African American ministers for a conference at Ebenezer Baptist Church in Atlanta in January 1957. They approved the proposal for the SCLC and elected King as its president. Because of Bayard's influence,

An interfaith/interracial group led the Prayer Pilgrimage for Freedom. Attracting about 25,000 demonstrators, it could be considered a "dress rehearsal" for the 1963 March on Washington.

King now headed a civil rights organization that would carry out direct action campaigns for the next decade.

Building on the Montgomery victory, Bayard began new campaigns right away. In February 1957, he had King and other leaders send a telegram to President Dwight D. Eisenhower, urging him to speak in the South supporting the *Brown* decision and condemning recent bombings.

Eisenhower refused.

King enlisted Bayard to organize a "Prayer Pilgrimage" to Washington, DC. Bayard was thrilled with his new responsibility. He had wanted to organize a March on Washington for African Americans since he first joined A. Philip Randolph's March on Washington Movement in 1941.

Held on May 17, 1957, the third anniversary of the *Brown* decision, the Prayer Pilgrimage for Freedom went beautifully, with

In 1957, Arkansas Governor Orval Faubus sent armed troops to block nine African American children from enrolling at all-white Central High School in Little Rock, Arkansas. President Eisenhower sent federal troops to escort the black students into school and protect them for the rest of the school year.

25,000 demonstrators gathering at the Lincoln Memorial for a program of spirituals and speeches. Bayard scheduled King to be the last, and therefore the most important, speaker of the day. King rose to the occasion, delivering a rousing call to action. "Give us the ballot," he said, "and we will quietly and nonviolently, without rancor or bitterness, implement the Supreme Court's decision."[77] King's appearance at the Prayer Pilgrimage helped to establish him as a national civil rights leader.

It was exactly what Bayard had hoped for—recognition of the rise of King and nonviolent direct action as the most significant development in the new civil rights era. Thanks partly to Bayard, direct action was becoming the preferred method for advancing civil rights.

In the fall of 1958, Arkansas Governor Orval Faubus was threatening to close public schools in his state if the federal government tried to force them to integrate. In response, Bayard and Randolph announced plans for the interracial Youth March for Integrated Schools. Bayard took charge of organizing.

On October 25, 1958, 10,000 young people demonstrated for integrated schools by marching from Constitution Avenue to the Lincoln Memorial in Washington, DC. The march was so successful that Bayard organized another to take place on April 18, 1959. This time, 25,000 youths and activists took to the streets in Washington, many of them shouting, "Five, six, seven, eight, these United States must integrate!"[78]

Widely covered by the national media, the march was yet another major success for Bayard, and King took notice. King praised Bayard for his contacts with important people and his ability to raise money. He appreciated Bayard's organizational skills and abilities so much that he proposed hiring Bayard as the director of the SCLC. At least one member of the committee objected, stating that SCLC's enemies might use Bayard's 1953 arrest in California to "smear" SCLC.[79]

SCLC did not hire Bayard as director.

But Bayard had plenty of other work on his plate. He still had his job with the War Resisters League and his passion for world peace.

Bayard traveled to the Sahara desert in 1959 in an unsuccessful attempt to prevent France from testing nuclear weapons there. He returned to the United States to lay plans for yet another huge direct action campaign. But, as usual, more trouble was ahead.

In a series of debates, Bayard pitted the nonviolent struggle for racial integration against Malcolm X's calls for racial separatism and the use of "any means necessary," including violence, to pursue racial justice. Malcolm X is shown here in 1961 standing between Bayard and student leader Michael R. Winston.

OUTCAST

On June 9, 1960, Bayard, Randolph, and King held a press conference announcing a direct action campaign involving massive rallies outside the 1960 Republican and Democratic national conventions, where candidates for president were nominated. They called for the major political parties to support civil rights. King predicted that "more than 5,000 demonstrators" would march outside every session of the conventions.[81] The conventions—and the demonstrations—would be on televisions all over the country.

Not all civil rights leaders liked the idea. In a blistering letter to Randolph, NAACP leader Roy Wilkins wrote: "We do not believe a mass picket line which will clog entrances, irritate delegates and officials and possibly erupt into name-calling or disorder will advance the cause."[82] Democratic Representative Adam Clayton Powell, Jr., of Harlem, was afraid that the marches would hurt his status in the Democratic Party. He delivered a speech implying that immoral elements were influencing King. He then had an aide phone King with a vicious threat: Unless the marches were called off, Powell would leak a lie to the media that King and Bayard were romantically involved.[83]

Although Powell's threat rang hollow, King grew concerned. What if his close association with Bayard convinced people to believe the lie and, because of their own prejudices, withdraw their support for King and the civil rights movement?

King cut Bayard out of his inner circle of advisors, no longer calling him for advice, counsel, and wisdom, as he had done for nearly four years. Bayard was crushed. He had done so much for King, but now he was an outcast.

Depressed, Bayard struggled to regain his composure. He decided to rise up and focus on direct action campaigns for world peace. Early in 1961, he helped lead a 4,000-mile peace walk (with the help of a boat) from San Francisco to Moscow. In 1962, he traveled to Africa to assist with direct action campaigns for independence and to advise African leaders about the philosophy and tactics of nonviolence, just as he had done with King.

Despite this important work, Bayard missed being one of King's close advisors. He met regularly with Randolph in Harlem, where they continued to devise ways to advance the civil rights movement. In late 1962, Randolph proposed the idea of another march on Washington. Unlike those in the late 1950s, which focused on voting rights and school integration, this march would address the dire economic conditions of many African Americans, especially the lack of jobs. The idea captivated Bayard and he enlisted two trusted aides, Norman Hill and Tom Kahn, young democratic socialists who had worked with Bayard on the Youth Marches for Integrated Schools. The three of them began planning a "two-day action program" for June 1963.[84]

Even more exciting, Bayard and King were reconnecting. Without Bayard's presence in his inner circle, King's civil rights work had begun to flounder. King realized he really needed Bayard's abilities to organize, strategize, and make detailed plans. When King came calling, Bayard "lit up."[85] He did not need much convincing to return to King's circle of advisors. Like his grandmother, Bayard believed in forgiving those who had hurt him, including those who never sought forgiveness. He was ready, willing, and delighted to offer his service to King and the SCLC. He also hoped to convince King to participate in the march he was planning.

In 1963, the SCLC was waging a campaign against segregation in Birmingham, Alabama. As the nation watched on television news programs, children demonstrating for freedom were attacked

Television

Bayard saw television as an important tool in the nonviolent crusade for civil rights. It brought the struggle into people's homes in a way the newspapers never could. They could now see and hear protesters being attacked by police and jeering racist mobs. "With the coming of television, the violence of the South was no longer tucked away from the nation's attention," Bayard would later write. "As the camera laid bare the Southern lies, public opinion turned against the South."[86]

by police dogs and knocked over by high-pressure fire hoses. Compounding the nation's outrage was the tragic news that NAACP staffer Medgar Evers was murdered outside his home in Jackson, Mississippi, by a member of the White Citizens' Council.

The violence they saw on the televisions in their living rooms touched the hearts of many Americans and helped build sympathy for the civil rights struggle. A nonviolent march in Washington was the right tactic for this time, and King committed to the March.

With the momentum growing in the South, Bayard broadened the focus of the March to jobs *and* freedom and proposed that the major civil rights leaders unite behind a concrete list of demands and form a group to handle major issues related to the March. The group included Randolph, King, Roy Wilkins of the NAACP, John Lewis of the Student Nonviolent Coordinating Committee, Whitney Young of the National Urban League, and James Farmer of the Congress of Racial Equality. Collectively known as the "Big Six," they would need an executive director to recruit a staff and organize the many details involved in such a massive undertaking, which had been rescheduled for late August.

Bayard, of course, wanted to be this director. But not everyone agreed.

Randolph (center) was the director of the March, and he chose Bayard as his deputy.

"Rustin," John Lewis recalled, "really became the director of the March."[88]

chapter 17
MR. MARCH-ON-WASHINGTON

NAACP leader Roy Wilkins did not want Bayard to direct the March on Washington for Jobs and Freedom because of Bayard's past participation in the Young Communist League and his 1953 arrest in Pasadena. Wilkins thought it was too risky for Bayard to be appointed to a high-profile position.

After hearing of Wilkins's objection, three members of the Big Six—King, Lewis, and Farmer—decided to nominate Randolph for director and give him the power to choose his deputy. It was a clever move. Wilkins respected Randolph too much to oppose him, and they knew Randolph would name Bayard as his deputy. The plan worked. Wilkins agreed to the nomination, and Randolph immediately appointed Bayard as his deputy.[87]

Bayard was delighted, but there was no time to celebrate. The March on Washington for Jobs and Freedom was only eight weeks away!

The next two months were unbelievably busy. There were no cell phones or personal computers in 1963, so Bayard used index cards for planning and had fliers, leaflets, and posters printed to get the word out. Telephones rang constantly, with people requesting information, reporters seeking interviews, and civil rights leaders wondering about their roles in the March. The national headquarters

Bayard established the March's national headquarters in Harlem.

did not have an intercom or speaker system, so staff often resorted to shouting their messages from one office to another.

Bayard recruited a first-rate staff of young people committed to the cause. He made Tom Kahn his personal assistant. Norman Hill traveled around the country to work with local organizers. For transportation coordinator, he chose another assistant, Rachelle

Final Plans for the

MARCH ON WASHINGTON
FOR JOBS AND FREEDOM

AUGUST 28, 1963

This is the SECOND and LAST Organizing Manual of the MARCH ON WASHINGTON FOR JOBS AND FREEDOM

READ IT CAREFULLY. *There have been changes in arrangements* since the publication of Organizing Manual No. 1.

1. There will be NO separate state locations. All buses will proceed directly to the Washington Monument.

2. The NEW routes of March are Independence and Constitution Avenues.
(Read further for full details)

Distribute this manual today. Time is short. If you need additional copies, let us know TODAY!

MARCH ON WASHINGTON FOR JOBS AND FREEDOM
170 West 130th Street • New York, N.Y. 10027 • FI 8-1900

Cleveland Robinson
Chairman, Administrative Committee

Bayard Rustin
Deputy Director

Bayard and his staff wrote a detailed instruction manual for regional March leaders, providing specific directions to drivers and riders.

Horowitz, which surprised her because she did not know how to drive. Bayard knew she would be able to handle all the details, and she did. Her team arranged for 1,500 buses, 21 trains, and 3 planes to convey participants from across the nation. No one knew how many carloads would show up, or how many people would arrive on foot.

Marchers were instructed to bring peanut butter sandwiches, apples, cakes, and soft drinks—nothing that would spoil under the hot August sun. Three hundred volunteers in New York used five tons of American cheese to prepare 80,000 sandwiches for sack lunches. Also included were an apple and a piece of marble cake (light and dark batter swirled together—an appropriate dessert for the occasion). Hungry marchers could buy these lunches for fifty cents. Giant water tanks would supply 21 temporary water fountains.

Staffers also anticipated the possibility of sickness, instructing drivers to stock their buses with first-aid kits and extra water, and enlisting two hundred volunteer nurses and doctors to work at 25 first-aid stations. No detail was too small. Bayard and his staff even came up with the exact number of portable toilets required for the big day: 200.

Safety was a major concern. Bayard asked an African American sergeant in the New York Police Department to recruit and train hundreds of African American officers to police the March. As peacekeepers, they did not wear their uniforms and were armed only with walkie-talkies. Bayard led nonviolence training for these volunteers, instructing them to encircle troublemakers and escort them safely to police officers waiting outside the march area.

Key parts of Bayard's job were to publicize the March, educate participants about the need for nonviolence, and highlight the demands of the March—jobs and enforcement of constitutional rights. He stayed in touch with countless reporters, politicians, and government officials monitoring the high drama surrounding the March. The national headquarters sent out press releases to media across the country. The better informed everyone was, the smoother the March would be.

Getting everything right required long workdays for everyone. Sixteen-hour days and quick meals in the office were the norm, with some staff members even sleeping at the headquarters, too tired or busy to go home. But the excitement and energy kept everyone focused on the job.

One formidable opponent was South Carolina Senator Strom Thurmond. A longtime antagonist of the civil rights movement, he was now intent on derailing the March. Armed with information provided by the FBI, Thurmond announced on the Senate floor that Bayard was a communist orchestrating the March for anti-American propaganda purposes. Spurred by Thurmond, reporters asked Randolph if he intended to ask Bayard to resign. "No," Randolph replied. "Rustin is Mr. March-on-Washington himself."[89] King offered his support too, stating that Bayard was "a brilliant, efficient and dedicated organizer and one of the most persuasive interpreters of nonviolence."[90]

Thurmond would not give up. Producing more FBI material, the senator publicized Bayard's 1953 arrest in Pasadena, suggesting that a "pervert" was leading the March.[91] As newspapers around the country covered Thurmond's charge, the Big Ten (the Big Six had grown to include white labor and religious leaders) became more determined than ever to rally around Bayard.

The grandest defense came from Randolph, who spoke of his "complete confidence" in Bayard's "character, integrity, and extraordinary ability."[92] Later, Bayard remembered Randolph saying, "If Bayard, a homosexual, is that talented—and I know the work he does for me—maybe I should be looking for somebody else homosexual who could be so useful."[93]

Bayard kept his job, and Thurmond lost the battle. Just a few weeks away, the March was unstoppable.

Perhaps most rewarding, though, was the support Bayard received from his colleagues in the civil rights movement. In a letter, Bayard wrote: "It's nice to know that one has friends who will stand up and be counted when the time comes."[94] How different from the way he felt when King expelled him from his inner circle or when the FOR released him after his 1953 arrest. In a few short years, Bayard had come a long way, and so had his colleagues.

Some of the marchers linked arms, singing freedom songs like "We Shall Overcome," while others walked in silence.

King and the other Big Ten leaders trailed behind the front of the crowd, following the lead of their foot soldiers of the civil rights movement.

"I HAVE A DREAM"

On the morning of August 28th, Bayard arose early and walked to the Washington Monument, where the March would begin. He wanted to see the early results of eight weeks of intense planning. Surveying the march area around 6:00 a.m., he grew worried. Only a couple hundred marchers had arrived, hardly a good sign. When members of the press asked where all the people were, Bayard pulled a sheet of paper out of his pocket, checked his watch, and said: "Gentlemen, everything is going exactly according to plan."[95] He did not let them see that the paper was blank.

His worries soon disappeared. By 9:30 a.m., 40,000 marchers were gathered at the Washington Monument; ninety minutes later, the number had grown to 90,000. The marchers kept coming, and the excitement kept building as the crowd reached at least 250,000.

As the throngs awaited the March and rally, well known singers on the stage at the Lincoln Memorial inspired the crowd with freedom songs. Josh White, the blues man who had given Bayard a singing job decades before, gave beautiful expression to the spirit of the day, singing "Ain't nobody gonna stop me, nobody gonna keep me, from marchin' down freedom's road."[96] He was joined by famous athletes and Hollywood celebrities in a joyful celebration of freedom.

Some had feared the March would turn violent, but Bayard and hundreds of marshals made sure it was peaceful.

The march from the Washington Monument to the Lincoln Memorial began around noon. The program at the Lincoln Memorial started at 2:00 p.m. Opera singer Marian Anderson opened with the national anthem. Randolph, who had envisioned such a march more than twenty years before, delivered the first remarks. As the chief organizer, Bayard buzzed about like a stage director, making sure all the musicians and speakers were on time, in their places, and prepared with their lines. At one point, though, he simply stopped, stood next to the main podium, and smiled joyfully. That was near the end of the program, when legendary gospel singer Mahalia Jackson sang a breathtaking rendition of the spiritual "I've Been 'Buked and I've Been Scorned." With his own roots in spirituals, Bayard knew the music so well he quietly sang along as the Queen of Gospel moved the massive audience to tears.

Bayard's 23-year-old friend John Lewis delivered the most controversial and militant speech of the day. When the Archbishop of Washington, Rev. Patrick O'Boyle, previewed the text of Lewis's remarks, he demanded that it be edited or he would not deliver his invocation. Even toned down, Lewis's speech was fierce and strong, electrifying the crowd as none of the other speeches had.

Bayard scheduled King to speak last, as he had for the 1957 Prayer Pilgrimage. He knew that King, the Baptist preacher from Atlanta,

National Archives and Records Administration

John Lewis (second from right) had prepared a speech that some thought was too strongly worded. At the urging of A. Philip Randolph (seated next to Lewis), whom he greatly respected, Lewis agreed to remove phrases that recalled violent images from the Civil War. Other leaders of the March (left to right): Mathew Ahmann, National Catholic Conference for Interracial Justice; Cleveland Robinson, Chairman of the Demonstration Committee; Rabbi Joachim Prinz, American Jewish Congress; A. Philip Randolph; Joseph Rauh, Jr., a Washington, DC attorney; John Lewis, Student Nonviolent Coordinating Committee; and Floyd McKissick, Congress of Racial Equality.

had become the most powerful voice in the civil rights movement. As the last scheduled speaker, he would be the final exclamation point. King strode to the podium and silenced the 250,000 marchers, holding them spellbound with his powerful dream. "I have a dream that . . . one day right there in Alabama, little black boys

King's speech inspired the crowd to make his dream come alive back home in their communities.

and black girls will be able to join hands with little white boys and white girls as sisters and brothers. I have a dream today."[97] After he was finished sharing his dream, the sea of people standing in front of the Lincoln Memorial erupted in applause, cheers, smiles, and tears. It was to become King's most famous speech and a defining moment in history.

Then Bayard stepped to the podium to read the demands of the March. "Friends," he announced, "at five o'clock today the leaders whom you have heard will go to President Kennedy to carry the demands of this revolution. It is now time for you to act. I will read each demand and you will respond to it. So that when Mr. Wilkins and Dr. King and the other eight leaders go, they are carrying with them the demands which you have given your approval to." As he read each demand, he punctuated his words by thrusting his right arm into the air. "The first demand is that we have effective civil rights legislation, no compromise . . . and that it include public accommodations, decent housing, integrated education . . . and the right to vote. What do you say?"[98] Never before had he spoken to so many people. Never before had the civil rights leaders

Despite this crisis, reactionary Republicans and Southern Democrats in Congress are still working to defeat effective civil rights legislation. They fight against the rights of all workers and minority groups. They are sworn enemies of freedom and justice. They proclaim states rights in order to destroy human rights.

The Southern Democrats came to power by disfranchising the Negro. They know that as long as black workers are voteless, exploited, and underpaid, the fight of the white workers for decent wages and working conditions will fail. They know that semi-slavery for one means semi-slavery for all.

We march to demonstrate, massively and dramatically, our unalterable opposition to these forces—and to their century-long robbery of the American people. Our bodies, numbering over 100,000, will bear witness—to serve historic notice—that Jobs and Freedom are needed NOW.

WHAT WE DEMAND *

1. Comprehensive and effective *civil rights legislation* from the present Congress—without compromise or filibuster—to guarantee all Americans
    access to all public accommodations
    decent housing
    adequate and integrated education
    the right to vote

2. Withholding of Federal funds from all programs in which discrimination exists.

3. Desegregation of *all school districts in 1963.*

4. Enforcement of the *Fourteenth Amendment*—reducing Congressional representation of states where citizens are disfranchised.

5. A new *Executive Order* banning discrimination in all housing supported by federal funds.

6. Authority for the *Attorney General* to institute *injunctive suits* when any constitutional right is violated.

7. A massive federal program to train and place all unemployed workers—Negro and white—on meaningful and dignified jobs at decent wages.

8. A national *minimum wage* act that will give all Americans a decent standard of living. (Government surveys show that anything less than $2.00 an hour fails to do this.)

9. A broadened *Fair Labor Standards Act* to include all areas of employment which are presently excluded.

10. A federal *Fair Employment Practices Act* barring discrimination by federal, state, and municipal governments, and by employers, contractors, employment agencies, and trade unions.

*Support of the March does not necessarily indicate endorsement of every demand listed. Some organizations have not had an opportunity to take an official position on all of the demands advocated here.

4

HOW OUR DEMANDS WILL BE PRESENTED
TO CONGRESS

The March on Washington projects a new concept of lobbying.

For more than a century we have written to Congressmen and visited Presidents. For more than a century our leaders have walked in the legislative halls bearing petitions and appeals. For more than a century our experts have drafted and proposed far-sighted remedies for the diseases that beset our society.

Progress, if any, has been slow.

On August 28, our leaders will once again lay our demands before the powers of government. That morning, they will meet with the President and the leaders of both political parties. But in keeping with this new—and more profound—concept of lobbying, our 100,000 marchers will not go to Capitol Hill, nor to the White House.

Instead, we have invited every single Congressman and Senator to come to us—to hear our demands for jobs and freedom, NOW.

Reserved seats will await them at the Lincoln Memorial and we shall make public the names of those who attend.

The more than 100,000 Americans of all races and colors will serve historic notice to Congress and the entire nation that a profound change has taken place in the rapidly growing civil rights revolution.

Our demonstration—the largest and most significant in the history of Washington—will bear eloquent witness that we do not come to beg or plead for rights denied for centuries. Our massive March from the Washington Monument to Lincoln Memorial, our enormous rally at the Memorial, will speak out to Congress and the nation with a single voice—for jobs and freedom, NOW.

● For these reasons, there will be no separate state locations in Washington. All marchers will, instead, proceed directly on arrival to the Washington Monument.

● Do not seek appointments with your Senators and Representatives on Capitol Hill. This will make it more difficult for Congressmen to be present at the Lincoln Memorial programs.

● All buses *must* proceed directly to the Washington Monument without detour.

● Participating groups should not schedule separate meetings that day.

5

Bayard had included the demands of the March in the instruction manual.

stepped aside to make room for Bayard in such a public setting. Never before had he enjoyed such a prominent speaking role. This was clearly an important day, both for the country and for Bayard.

President Kennedy watched Bayard on television at the White House and eventually pledged to ensure that African Americans would soon enjoy the first class citizenship that was their birthright.

The 1963 March on Washington for Jobs and Freedom was the largest and most important nonviolent demonstration for civil rights in US history. As the 250,000 marchers walked away, beginning the long trek back to their home communities, Bayard spotted his mentor, Randolph, standing alone on the stage. "I could see he was tired," Bayard later said. "I said to him, 'Mister Randolph, it seems that your dream has come true.' And when I looked into his eyes, tears were streaming down his cheeks."[99]

Demonstrators march in Washington, DC, in memory of the girls who died in the Birmingham bombing.

NEGROES ARE LYING DEAD IN THE STREET

Addie Mae Collins, Carole Robertson, and Cynthia Wesley were 14 years old.

Denise McNair was only 11.

Eighteen days after the triumphant March on Washington, they were murdered.

White racists bombed the Sixteenth Street Baptist Church in Birmingham, Alabama, killing the four young black girls attending Sunday school.

Shocked and angry, Bayard organized a Day of Mourning. Rather than calling for demonstrators from across the country to come to one location, Bayard asked them to march in silence wearing black armbands or ribbons in their local communities. More than 10,000 people gathered in New York City to protest the murders of the four children and all violence against African Americans. Bayard delivered a fiery speech at the protest, demanding that the federal government protect African Americans struggling for civil rights. The crowd cheered when Bayard called "for an uprising, nonviolently, in 100 cities, where we will sit and stand and stand and sit and go to jail and jail again, until there are no color barriers."[100]

President Kennedy had proposed legislation to end racial discrimination, but before it could get through Congress, he was

The Harlem riots lasted three long nights and spread to Brooklyn.

assassinated. His successor, President Lyndon Johnson, saw to it that the law was passed, and he signed the Civil Rights Act on July 2, 1964.

Yet the nightmare of violence continued. Two weeks after the Civil Rights Act was signed, an off-duty New York police officer shot and killed an African American teenager. Thousands of Harlem's residents exploded in anger. Running through the streets, they broke windows, destroyed property, and set fires. The police responded by chasing them, beating them, and shooting at them.

Bayard was furious with both the police brutality and the

The Harlem riots left one person dead, 150 people injured, and 500 people arrested.

violence committed by Harlem residents. He rushed to his old neighborhood to try to restore peace. When he asked Harlem residents to put their guns away and rely on nonviolence, a chorus of boos and jeers rang out. They spat on him and shouted insults and threats as he tried to lead a peaceful march. Harlem residents were so sick of police harassment that Bayard's call for nonviolence no longer seemed relevant.

Things got violent again, this time in Alabama, where African Americans planned to march 50 miles from Selma to Montgomery, the state capital, to demand the right to vote. The 525 peaceful

Bayard, shown here at the Harlem riots, opposed the increasingly popular belief that African Americans should fight for their freedom by using any means necessary, including violence.

marchers only got as far as a bridge on the outskirts of Selma, where police officers, some on horseback, attacked them with clubs and tear gas. Many marchers collapsed with serious injuries on the street while some were able to escape the beatings and run to safety. This display of police brutality was broadcast across the country on television. That day, March 7, 1965, came to be known as "Bloody Sunday."

The Right to Vote

The Fifteenth Amendment to the Constitution granted African Americans the right to vote in 1870. Just as later Supreme Court decisions did not necessarily result in desegregation, the constitutional right to vote did not make it easy to cast a ballot. Election officials throughout the South prevented most African Americans from registering to vote. Sometimes they required African Americans to pass "literacy tests," difficult exams about history, or even answer ridiculous questions like "How many bubbles are in a bar of soap?"[103] Poll taxes required people to pay to vote, and often did not apply to white voters. Some, including White Citizens' Councils and the Ku Klux Klan, threatened physical harm and even murder if black citizens tried to register to vote.

Back in Harlem, Bayard led a rally supporting the marchers in their struggle for the right to vote. He also advised King about the best way to respond to the violence. On March 21, 1965, 8,000 people left Selma. By the time they reached Montgomery on March 25, the crowd had grown to 25,000. Bayard and Randolph joined many others at the steps of the state capitol building when King spoke these words: "Our aim must never be to defeat or humiliate the white man, but to win his friendship and understanding. We must come to see that the end we seek is a society at peace with itself, a society that can live with its conscience. And that will be a day not of the white man, not of the black man. That will be the day of man as man."[101]

The Selma to Montgomery march paved the way for the passage of the Voting Rights Act of 1965, ensuring African Americans the right to vote without harassment or intimidation. Bayard was at the White House when President Johnson signed the historic legislation—a victorious day for all the nonviolent marchers.

However, five days after President Johnson signed the Voting Rights Act, another riot erupted. In Watts, a mostly African American and poor neighborhood in Los Angeles, a white police officer arrested a young African American man suspected of driving while intoxicated. A tense crowd gathered at the scene, and a

Credit the Library of Congress

Bayard (lower left) organized northern "solidarity" demonstrations to build support for marchers attempting a peaceful march from Selma to Montgomery, AL in 1965.

violent exchange between the officers and the crowd triggered a six-day riot. Rioters set fires, smashed windows, overturned cars, and looted stores. California's governor sent 14,000 troops to the area in an attempt to reestablish order, and by the end of the rioting, 34 people lay dead and approximately 1,000 were injured. More than 4,000 African Americans were arrested.

Bayard accompanied King around the devastated neighborhood of Watts, surveying the damage and talking with some of the rioters. When a young man announced the rioters had "won," Bayard said: "How have you won? Homes have been destroyed, Negroes are lying dead in the streets, the stores [where] you buy food and clothes are destroyed." The young rioter replied: "We won because we made the whole world pay attention to us."[102] It seemed that nonviolence was losing its appeal, particularly in urban areas outside of the South.

Bayard and King left Watts believing the riots stemmed in part from the neighbor-hood's dire economic circumstances. Poor, jobless, and alienated from mainstream society, the residents had had enough. They just exploded.

The war continued to rage in Vietnam, and disagreements about anti-war protests drove Bayard and King apart.

chapter 20

WE WILL TRY OUR BEST TO CARRY ON

Bayard saw that the root causes of urban violence were poverty, desperation, and hopelessness. Three of his mentors, Randolph, Muste, and Norman Thomas, also recognized that once equality under law was achieved, the larger struggle would be for a livable wage, decent schools, and health care for all. So in 1964, the A. Philip Randolph Institute was founded to address these problems, with Bayard as executive director.

While he worked at the Randolph Institute, Bayard continued to advise King on civil rights matters, but he found himself increasingly at odds with King over three major issues: the Vietnam War, the concept of Black Power, and the fight against poverty.

The Vietnam War

The conflict in Vietnam, a small country in Southeast Asia, pitted a pro-communist government in the North against an anti-communist government in the South. Supporting the anti-communist forces, the United States had sent military advisors to the country as early as 1950, but over time the US government also began sending combat forces. During the Johnson administration, the number of combat troops on the ground peaked, and film footage appeared nightly on the television news, bringing the war into America's living rooms.

At a 1965 rally in New York to protest the Vietnam War, Bayard told 17,000 protesters to "take to the streets" and, with other speakers, led 2,000 marchers to the United Nations to protest the war.[104] To Bayard and his pacifist friends, the notion of building peace through waging war was inconsistent, immoral, and destined to fail. Bayard also advised King, who had been awarded the 1964 Nobel Peace Prize, to take a public stand against the war.

As the war progressed, however, Bayard disagreed with the proposals of some of his anti-war colleagues who seemed interested only in ending US involvement there. He wanted both sides to "stop the killing" and negotiate a settlement, not merely to "bring the boys home."

After 1965, Bayard encouraged King to be cautious when speaking about the war. He now believed that if King linked the civil rights movement to the peace movement, he would lose the backing of those who supported the Vietnam War.

King disagreed, especially after he saw a photograph of a Vietnamese child killed by the US military. The graphic image disturbed him so much that he felt he could no longer be silent about the war. He was also angry that young African American soldiers were dying on the battlefields at a rate much higher than white soldiers. King began to speak out publicly against the war, and in April 1967 he led a peace march from Central Park to the United Nations.

Bayard was not by his side.

The gap between Bayard and King widened over the issue of Black Power, which surfaced most visibly in 1966. King and Stokely Carmichael, the new chairman of the Student Nonviolent Coordinating Committee (SNCC), participated in a march across Mississippi for voting rights. Although it remained nonviolent, this protest had a noticeably different feel, partly because at a rally in Greenwood, Mississippi, Carmichael encouraged the crowd to chant, "We want Black Power!"[105] As the crowd repeated the phrase again and again, their anger seemed to mount.

Not long after the Greenwood rally, SNCC called for an all-black civil rights struggle that was willing to use violent methods. This appeal fractured the movement. On one side were Bayard, Randolph, King, and Wilkins of the NAACP, who continued to favor achieving integration through nonviolence. On the other, Carmichael and the young militants of the new Black Power movement seemed to embrace racial separatism and the threat of violence to achieve their ends. Although Bayard and King agreed that Black Power was a controversial idea, they disagreed about the best way to respond to it. Bayard often criticized Black Power in public, and in October 1966 he placed an advertisement in *The New York Times* denouncing Black Power's threat of violence and racial separatism. Bayard asked King to join other civil rights leaders in signing the advertisement. King not only refused; he also publicly criticized Bayard's efforts.

Bayard and King also disagreed about the best way to solve the problem of poverty. Near the end of 1966, Bayard and the Randolph Institute proposed "A Freedom Budget for All Americans," a $185 billion budget plan designed to eliminate poverty and joblessness and improve living conditions (housing, education, and healthcare) for the nation's poor.

Bayard envisioned the Freedom Budget as a program to advance the civil rights movement "from protest to politics."[106] He no longer saw direct action techniques as the best way to advance civil rights in all circumstances. The time had come, he said, for citizens to vote and to demand civil rights laws and anti-poverty programs from elected officials.

Some of Bayard's colleagues in the radical pacifist movement were perplexed, even angry, when they saw that the Freedom Budget did not cut military spending. Just as he had advised King not to speak out against the Vietnam War so that he would not lose support for civil rights by those who favored the war, Bayard believed that if the budget called for military cuts, supporters of the war would not vote for the budget in Congress. The harsh truth was that the Vietnam War was so costly that there was virtually no chance for the budget to win in Congress anyway.

Near the end of 1967, King, still believing in the need for direct action, called for thousands of poor people of all colors to go to Washington to demand jobs, health care, education, and other basic necessities. During this "Poor People's Campaign," protesters would pitch tents on the Washington Mall, take their demands to the offices of politicians, and practice civil disobedience by sitting in at Congress and in city streets.

Warning of violence, Bayard did not offer his support for the campaign. "I seriously question the efficacy of Dr. King's plans for

On April 8, 1968, Coretta Scott King (center) and major civil rights, labor, and religious leaders led a silent march supporting the sanitation workers in Memphis and honoring the life and legacy of Martin Luther King, Jr. Bayard can be seen behind Ralph Abernathy (in the light coat) and Andrew Young.

the April march," Bayard told a reporter in February 1968.[107] King had appreciated Bayard's advice, given in private, but felt betrayed when he publicly aired his criticisms. Bayard, in turn, no longer felt welcome at strategy sessions with King.

These were difficult days for Bayard. He and King had grown apart in many ways. Old friends saw him as an enemy. The war was draining the resources needed to transform society and violence was on the rise worldwide. Things were about to get even worse.

On April 4, 1968, King was preparing for an event in support of a sanitation workers' strike for better job security and benefits. As he stood alone on the balcony of the Lorraine Motel in Memphis, Tennessee, he was shot and killed by James Earl Ray, a white high school dropout and escaped convict.

Bayard was devastated. The next morning he boarded a plane for Memphis, but once airborne he learned the plane would be landing in Washington, DC. President Johnson had called an emergency meeting with civil rights leaders. The president was especially concerned about the possibility of violence breaking out in cities across the country.

After finally arriving in Memphis, Bayard organized the nonviolent march King had hoped to lead. He announced to the press that

King's murder sparked race riots in more than a hundred cities, including Washington, DC, shown here.

the best way to honor King was by recognizing human rights and establishing economic justice for people of all colors.

The days following King's death were painful. African Americans in the nation's inner cities were lashing out in anger and frustration, and no one was quite sure how to proceed. "Martin's death," Bayard wrote in a letter, "leaves a fantastic vacuum that nobody—not me and ten others combined—could fill. We will try our best to carry on, though."[108]

Coretta Scott King enlisted her husband's best friend, Rev. Ralph David Abernathy, to take charge of the SCLC. Bayard volunteered to help lead the Poor People's Campaign, but when personality and tactical differences erupted between him and the SCLC, he stepped down.

Still, Bayard soldiered on, but it was not easy. The historic civil rights movement that King had led from 1955 to 1968 was floundering, unsure of a new direction. Many of Bayard's colleagues in the radical peace movement thought he was a traitor to the cause of world peace. His mentor, A. Philip Randolph, though he was still respected, was no longer the mighty warrior he once was. These were lonely days, but Bayard did not despair. He wrote that "to remain human and to fulfill my commitment to a just society, I must continue to fight for the liberation of all." No matter how difficult life was, Bayard had no plans to desert the "great cause" of human freedom.[109]

Bayard became good friends with Golda Meir, Israel's first female prime minister. Known as a fierce and tough woman, Meir once made Bayard chicken soup when he was suffering from a cold.

chapter 21
FIGHTING FOR ALL

By 1969, Bayard had been imprisoned more than twenty times. His enemies had assaulted him along the way, and death threats had not been uncommon. "I have been in a bombed church," he wrote. "My best friends, closest associates, and colleagues in arms have been beaten and assassinated."[110] The work was dangerous and difficult, both intellectually and physically.

After his Aunt Bessie saw him in 1971, she wrote him a letter urging him to take care of himself. "You are so busy and so much in demand," she wrote. "I am much concerned about you. You seem depressed, not as jolly or as happy as you used to be."[111]

By the end of the year, Bayard suffered a heart attack requiring months of rest.

Once he had regained his health, Bayard worked hard to promote democracy and human rights in Chile, Paraguay, El Salvador, Grenada, Haiti, Lebanon, Poland, Zimbabwe, and South Africa. Bayard worked with an organization that investigated the oppression of Jews in the Soviet Union and he became an outspoken supporter of the Jewish state of Israel.

He also became passionate about helping refugees—women, men, and children who fled to another country as a way to escape war, violence, or oppression. He visited refugee camps in Africa,

Walter Naegle

Bayard with Archbishop Desmond Tutu in South Africa. Bayard wanted to see the end of the *white dictatorship* of apartheid in South Africa, but he wanted it replaced with a democratic, multiracial system, not with a *black dictatorship*.

Latin America, and Southeast Asia. Bayard wrote, "the camps are overcrowded, children are ill-fed, and the sick are inadequately cared for. But worst of all, these people—who face almost certain death if they return home—lack hope."[112] Back home, he urged political leaders to send supplies and money to the camps, and to make it possible for refugees to resettle in the United States.

In the early evening of April 13, 1977, Bayard returned to New York from Memphis, where he had led a pro-labor demonstration.

On his trips to refugee camps, Bayard paid special attention to the children. Trying to bring a little happiness to their day, he enjoyed singing and dancing with them.

He stood at the corner of Times Square and 42nd Street, waiting for a streetlight to change. He struck up a conversation with a man who was also waiting for the light, on his way to a nearby store.

The conversation lasted for hours. They got along so well that Walter Naegle became Bayard's closest companion for the rest of his life.

Walter played a special role in Bayard's life. He helped Bayard reconnect with long-lost friends, especially the radical pacifists who had dismissed him as a *sell out* during the Vietnam War. Walter also encouraged Bayard to meet with those asking him to speak out on behalf of gay rights. Although Bayard had championed various social movements throughout his life, he was not a visible presence in the gay rights movement until late in his life. But as a human rights activist, Bayard also believed it was the right thing for him to do, whether he was gay or straight; rights to life and liberty, he knew, belonged to all people. As he wrote in a letter, "My activism did not spring from my being gay, or for that matter, from my being

With all his travel and challenging work, Bayard longed for a steady companion, something he had not had for any extended period in his life. That changed when he met Walter Naegle.

black. Rather it is rooted, fundamentally, in my Quaker upbringing and the values that were instilled in me by my grandparents who reared me. Those values are based on the concept of a single human family and the belief that all members of that family are equal."[113]

Bayard began his advocacy on this issue by speaking to gay rights groups in the early 1980s, often suggesting that eliminating discrimination and prejudice against gays and lesbians was now the most important step for advancing human rights in the United States. As he put it, "if you want to know whether today people believe in democracy . . . if you want to know whether they are human rights activists, the question to ask is, 'What about gay people?' Because that is now the litmus paper by which this democracy is to be judged."[114]

He ramped up his involvement in the movement in 1985, when he urged Mayor Ed Koch and the New York City Council to pass legislation making it illegal to discriminate against gays and lesbians. Drawing from his own life experiences, he stated that "history

132

Stonewall, Gay Pride, and Gay Rights

In 1969, there were few places where homosexuals could gather. Some bars, like the Stonewall Inn in the Greenwich Village neighborhood of New York City, welcomed gay customers. Gay bars were frequently raided by police, who arrested customers. Stonewall was raided in the early morning hours of June 28. After suffering years of harassment from police, patrons of Stonewall had had enough. A crowd gathered, and a riot ensued. This event is viewed as the beginning of the gay rights movement.

On the one-year anniversary of the raid, Greenwich Village hosted the first Gay Pride Parade. Cities across the country held their own Gay Pride Parades, and within two years, gay rights organizations formed in every major city. Gays and lesbians celebrated their culture and fought for their civil rights.

In 1973, the American Psychiatric Association removed homosexuality from its list of mental disorders.

demonstrates that no group is ultimately safe from prejudice, bigotry, and harassment so long as any group is subject to special negative treatment."[115]

To Bayard, it didn't matter which group was being discriminated against—all discrimination was wrong. As he said in an interview, "if we want to do away with the injustice to gays it will not be done because we get rid of the injustice to gays. It will be done because we are forwarding the effort for the elimination of injustice to all. And we will win the rights for gays, or blacks, or Hispanics, or women within the context of whether we are fighting for all."[116]

In the last years of his life, organizations and universities bestowed numerous honors and awards on Bayard for his many years of dedication to civil and human rights. He had never earned a college degree, but he was now receiving honorary degrees from the nation's top universities. But Bayard did not accept all award offers that came his way. In 1980, he declined an honorary degree from Yeshiva University because he disagreed with the university's refusal to bargain with a labor union begun by its faculty members.

Bayard was not lonely in the last years of his life. He and Walter

Bayard in Trafalgar Square, London, England.

spent a lot of time together, listening to music, cooking for friends, and traveling. Of course, it was not possible for them to get married at the time. (Massachusetts became the first state to issue marriage licenses to same-sex couples in 2004.) In order to gain some of the legal rights denied them because they could not marry, Bayard legally adopted Walter.

The two also worked together, and in July 1987, four months after Bayard's seventy-fifth birthday, they traveled to Haiti to investigate the country's preparations for upcoming democratic elections. Back in New York in late July, Bayard began to suffer from abdominal pains. On August 21, his pain got much worse and Walter took him to the hospital, where doctors discovered that Bayard's appendix had burst. The doctors performed emergency surgery, but Bayard died of a heart attack three days later.

In October, his friends gathered together for a memorial service at the Community Church in New York City. Bayard's longtime close friend, John Lewis, the former SNCC chairman, recently elected to the US Congress, spoke at the service. Lewis began his remarks with a simple statement that brought warm smiles to those familiar with Bayard's lifetime dedication to creative troublemaking: "Bayard Rustin! Oh, what a life!"[117]

Bayard Rustin High School, West Chester, PA, opened in 2006."

Bayard Rustin High School, West Chester, PA

chapter 22

LET FREEDOM RING

Motivated by his Quaker values, Bayard refused to stand by while other humans suffered, yet he himself suffered because of the bigotry of others. His accomplishments went largely unrecognized because he was forced to work behind the scenes. After his death, Bayard began to get more of the public recognition he deserved.

Residents in his hometown of West Chester, Pennsylvania, created a bold plan to honor Bayard for his significant contributions to world peace and civil rights. In May of 2002, the High School Name Committee of the West Chester Area School District decided to name a new high school after Bayard. But the plan encountered an obstacle when a member of the committee read an article that mentioned Bayard's time in prison for refusing to serve in World War II. And that he was gay.

The school board received a petition signed by 550 people objecting to naming the sixty-seven million dollar school after Bayard. The committee decided to investigate and asked for input from the community. They got it. On the evening of November 20, five hundred people came to a meeting at Stetson Middle School in West Chester to voice their opinions about Bayard Rustin. Community members were allowed three minutes to state their opinions. Most were in favor of Bayard Rustin High School, but about a quarter of them objected.

"Choosing a name for this school is about naming it after some-one we want our children to be proud of. Rustin was . . . a disgrace to America," said one speaker.[118] Some said Bayard was a communist, un-American, or a traitor. Some objected because he broke the law, and some protested because he was gay.

Eventually the committee decided to stick with their decision, stating in their report, "We have not seen, read, or heard anything that would give us reason to change our recommendation for the name of the new high school. The more we learned, the more we were convinced that Rustin is the right name."[119] The school board approved by a 6-3 vote.

Bayard Rustin High School opened in September of 2006 in the mostly white, politically conservative school district of West Chester.

Other exciting events took place. West Chester University held a two-day conference on Bayard in 1999 that brought together authors, activists, and friends, including Congressman John Lewis, to discuss Bayard's life and legacy. Three years later it established The Bayard Rustin Award for Compassion and Courage. In 2014, the university welcomed Walter to accept an Honorary Doctor of Public Service degree on Bayard's behalf. One year before, nearby Cheyney University had awarded Bayard an honorary Doctor of Humane Letters.

In September of 2010, the Board of Directors of the AFSC agreed that Bayard's name should be restored to the list of authors of *Speak Truth to Power*, their 1955 booklet about the mounting power strug-gle in the Cold War between the United States and the Soviet Union. When the publication was reissued in 2012, it included Bayard's name and added a historical note acknowledging his contributions to the document, along with an apology.

Books, theatrical productions, and films about Bayard began to appear after his death. *Brother Outsider: The Life of Bayard Rustin*, an award-winning documentary film, premiered on the Public Broadcasting System and has been seen by more than a million people.

On August 28, 2013, exactly fifty years after the March on Washington for Jobs and Freedom, a crowd gathered on the National Mall, between the Washington Monument and the Lincoln Memorial, just as they had in 1963. This time it was a celebration of the anniversary of the March, a ceremony called "Let Freedom Ring."

This time, the Washington Monument was caged in scaffolding, as workers repaired damage from an earthquake two years earlier. Tens of thousands of people waited in line at security checkpoints. Metal barriers kept them from getting near enough to the reflecting pool to dip a toe in. Plastic ponchos and umbrellas shielded spectators and speakers from a light rain.

This time dozens of speakers addressed the crowd for over four hours. Most of them invoked King's legacy, but many also acknowledged Bayard's role in the March and in the civil rights movement, including Kristin Stoneking, executive director of the Fellowship of Reconciliation. "His life commitment to nonviolence as a spiritual discipline exemplifies that pacifism is anything but passive," she proclaimed. "He refused to accept . . . society's expectation that he be straight; he refused to be at war with another nation by being imprisoned as a conscientious objector during World War II; and he refused to be at war with humanity by not accepting diminishment or divisions based on race." She urged the group to resist racism and militarism and "embrace the way of Rustin, the way of King, the way of nonviolence and peace."[120]

Some who attended that day had been there fifty years before, when King electrified the crowd with his "I have a dream" speech. John Lewis had been there. In fact, John Lewis, now in his 27th year as a US Congressman, was the only surviving speaker from the 1963 March. He spoke, as did many of the speakers, of both the progress that had been made in fifty years and the work that was yet to be done. "Too many of us still believe our differences define us instead of the divine spark that runs through all of human creation." Lewis recalled the words of A. Philip Randolph, saying "we may have come here on different ships, but we are all in the same boat now. So it doesn't matter whether they're black or white, Latino, Asian American, or Native American, whether we are gay or straight. We are one people. We are one family."[121]

This time the president did not watch the March on television in the White House. President Barack Obama was there. Former Presidents Jimmy Carter and Bill Clinton were there, as well. Carter recalled awarding King's Presidential Medal of Freedom to his widow, Coretta. He noted that many thought King had worked just

President Obama handed the Presidential Medal of Freedom to Walter Naegle as an aide announced, "Fifty years after the March on Washington he organized, America honors Bayard Rustin as one of its greatest architects for social change and a fearless advocate for its most vulnerable citizens."

to free African American people, "when in truth, he helped to free all people."[122]

Clinton recalled watching the March on television in Arkansas when he was 17 years old. He noted that there were still inequalities, but that "[t]he choice remains as it was on that distant summer day fifty years ago: cooperate and thrive or fight with each other and fall behind."[123]

The final speaker of the day was Barack Obama, America's first African American President. He spoke of those who had worked nonviolently for civil rights. "In the face of hatred, they prayed for their tormentors. In the face of violence, they stood up and sat in with the moral force of nonviolence. Willingly, they went to jail to protest unjust laws, their cells swelling with the sound of freedom songs." Obama thanked those who marched, saying "America became more free and more fair, not just for African Americans but for women and Latinos, Asians and Native Americans, for Catholics, Jews, and Muslims, for gays, for Americans with disabilities."[124]

Earlier that month, Obama had announced that Bayard would be awarded a posthumous Presidential Medal of Freedom for his life's work, and especially for his masterful organization of what King had called "the greatest demonstration for freedom in the history of our nation." The medal is the highest honor presented to civilians and was first awarded by President John F. Kennedy fifty years earlier. Walter Naegle received a call from Valerie Jarrett, the president's special assistant, informing him of the award and inviting him to receive it. On November 20, 2013, he arrived at the White House to accept the medal on Bayard's behalf.

The 16 recipients of the 2013 medal included feminist writer Gloria Steinem; singer Loretta Lynn; Oprah Winfrey; C.T. Vivian, a colleague of Bayard's from the civil rights movement; and former President Bill Clinton. Before the ceremony, Steinem, who had known Bayard, commented that the presentation of the award to her, C.T. Vivian, and Bayard was a testimony to the significance of the social movements of the 1960s and '70s, and their invaluable contributions to the expansion of our democracy.

At the ceremony Obama stood at the podium, introducing the recipients. Walter sat in a chair behind the president, next to Tam O'Shaughnessy, the life partner of astronaut Sally Ride, the first American woman in space. Posthumous medals had been awarded in the past, but were presented to widows, children, or other relatives of the deceased recipient. Tam O'Shaughnessy and Walter Naegle were different. For the first time, the Presidential Medal of Freedom was presented to the surviving same-sex partners of recipients, a sign of the progress our country has made in affirming the dignity and equality of those relationships. In the audience, Bayard's relatives and friends as well as West Chester's Mayor Carolyn Committa beamed as this long overdue recognition of Bayard took place.

When it came time for Obama to speak about Bayard, he started with the story of the blank piece of paper Bayard had consulted at the March on Washington to assure the press that everything was going according to plans. "Bayard had an unshakable optimism, nerves of steel, and, most importantly, a faith that if the cause is just and people are organized, nothing can stand in our way," the president continued. "For decades, this great leader, often at Dr. King's side, was denied his rightful place in history because he was openly gay. No medal can change that, but today, we honor Bayard Rustin's memory by taking our place in his march towards true equality, no matter who we are or who we love."[125]

From West Chester to the White House—Bayard had come a long way.

While he appreciated all the awards and recognition during his own lifetime, Bayard continued to believe that we have a long way to go in the march for freedom. The recognition was less important to him than the work. When he was a student at West Chester High School, Bayard wrote this poem.

I ask of you no shining gold;
I seek not epitaph or fame;
No monument of stone for me,
For man need never speak my name.

But when my flesh doth waste away
And seeds from stately trees do blow,
I pray that in my fertile clay
You gently let a small seed grow.

That seed, I pray, be evergreen
That in my dust may always be
That everlasting life and joy
You manifest in that green tree.[126]

Bayard's work toward obtaining equal rights for all came naturally from his belief in the equality of every member of the human family. He believed that whenever anyone or anything seeks to oppress or enslave us we can and should believe in ourselves and our abilities, and use nonviolence to resist injustice and relieve misery. Bayard's work is not finished. It is up to us, the human family, to continue the march toward freedom for all.

THINGS TO THINK ABOUT

If Bayard were alive today, what issues would he be concerned with?

What do you think is the bravest thing Bayard did?

Did Bayard do anything that shocked or surprised you?

Give some modern examples of nonviolent direct action that you have participated in, witnessed, or heard about.

Where do you see a need for more fairness in the world? How do you think a nonviolent movement could help make that happen?

Is there something you believe in so strongly that you would protest for it? Is there anything you would go to jail for? Why?

In 1986, Bayard gave a speech in which he said "gay people are the new barometer for social change. . . . The question of social change should be framed with the most vulnerable group in mind: gay people." Do you think that was true in 1986? Who do you think is the most vulnerable group today?

What do you think Bayard meant when he said we need "angelic troublemakers"?

How would Bayard's life have been different if he had been born in Mississippi instead of Pennsylvania?

How would Bayard's life have been different if he had been born fifty years later?

Bayard and Gandhi never met. What would they have talked about if they had?

If you could ask Bayard one question, what would it be?

IMPORTANT EVENTS IN BAYARD RUSTIN'S LIFE

Other important events in the civil rights movement appear in *italics*.

DATE EVENT

1912   Born in West Chester, PA

1932   Graduated from West Chester High School

1932   Enrolled in Wilberforce University

1934   Enrolled in Cheyney State Teachers College

1937   AFSC Peace Brigade

1937   Expelled from Cheyney State Teachers College

1937   Moved to Harlem

1938   Joined Young Communist League

1941   Joined A. Philip Randolph's March on Washington Movement

1941   Joined A.J. Muste's Fellowship of Reconciliation

1942   Arrested and beaten for sitting in white section of bus

1944   *Irene Morgan arrested on a bus*

1944   Arrested for refusing to report for military physical

1946   *Interstate bus segregation unconstitutional (Morgan v. Virginia)*

1946   Released from prison

1947   Journey of Reconciliation

1947   *Gandhi's nonviolent campaign won independence for India*

1948   *Mohandas Gandhi assassinated*

1948   World Pacifist meeting in India

1949   Served 22 days on a chain gang in North Carolina

1952   *African National Congress began nonviolent protest of apartheid*

1952   Visited Nigeria and Gold Coast (Ghana)

1953   Arrested in Pasadena, California, on morals charge

DATE EVENT

1954 *Brown vs. Board of Education ruling against school segregation*

1955 *Rosa Parks arrested on bus in Montgomery, Alabama*

1955 AFSC's *Speak Truth to Power* published (without Bayard's name)

1955 Arrested for protesting "Operation Alert"

1956 Assisted Martin Luther King, Jr. with Montgomery bus boycott

1957 Southern Christian Leadership Conference (SCLC) formed

1957 Prayer Pilgrimage for Freedom

1958 First Youth March for Integrated Schools

1958 Protest in London and Aldermaston, England, against nuclear weapons

1959 Second Youth March for Integrated Schools

1959 Sahara Project protesting France's testing of nuclear weapons

1960 King cut Bayard from his circle of advisors

1961 *Freedom Rides*

1961 4,000-mile peace walk from San Francisco to Moscow

1962 Debated Malcolm X

1963 March on Washington for Jobs and Freedom

1963 *16th Street Baptist Church in Birmingham bombed, killing four girls*

1964 *Harlem riots*

1964 *Civil Rights Act passed*

1964 A. Philip Randolph Institute formed with Bayard as executive director

1965 *Voting Rights Act passed*

1965 *Watts riot*

1965 Spoke against the Vietnam War

1966 A. Philip Randolph Institute proposed Freedom Budget

1966 Placed ad in New York Times denouncing "Black Power"

1967 *King proposed Poor People's Campaign*

1968 *Martin Luther King, Jr. assassinated*

1971 Heart attack

1977 Met Walter Naegle

1978 Traveled to Thailand to help refugees

1986 Testified for gay rights bill in New York City

1987 Died in New York City

2013 Awarded Presidential Medal of Freedom

ENDNOTES

The books cited in the following notes include many other helpful sources about Bayard and his life—interviews, news articles, even essays and letters written by Bayard. We encourage you to explore these sources as you continue to study Bayard's life and times.

1. Martin Luther King, Jr., "I Have A Dream," August 28, 1963, Washington, D.C. See online at **http://mlk-kpp01.stanford.edu/kingweb/publications/ speeches/address_at_march_on_washington.pdf**

2. John D'Emilio, *Lost Prophet: The Life and Times of Bayard Rustin* (New York: Free Press, 2003), pp. 11 and 14.

3. D'Emilio, *Lost Prophet*, p. 8.

4. Jervis Anderson, *Bayard Rustin: Troubles I've Seen* (New York: HarperCollins, 1997), p. 24.

5. "The Reminiscences of Bayard Rustin," November 14, 1984. Fourteen interviews with Bayard Rustin, November 14, 1984 through June 18, 1987. Columbia University Oral History Project, Columbia University, New York, NY.

6. Anderson, *Bayard Rustin*, p. 24.

7. "The Reminiscences of Bayard Rustin," November 14, 1984.

8. "The Reminiscences of Bayard Rustin," November 14, 1984.

9. William Still, *The Underground Railroad: A Record Of Facts, Authentic Narratives, Letters, ETC., Narrating The Hardships, Hair-Breadth Escapes And Death Struggles Of The Slaves In Their Efforts For Freedom, As Related By Themselves And Others, Or Witnessed By The Author*, 1872. See online at **http://www.gutenberg.org/ catalog/world/readfile?fk_files=3276649&pageno=1**

10. Anderson, *Bayard Rustin*, p. 25.

11. Anderson, *Bayard Rustin*, p. 26.

12. Anderson, *Bayard Rustin*, p. 26.

13. Anderson, *Bayard Rustin*, p. 27.

14. Anderson, *Bayard Rustin*, p. 27.

15. D'Emilio, *Lost Prophet*, p. 17.

16. D'Emilio *Lost Prophet*, p. 20.

17. "Cupid's Winter Message," *Garnet and White*, 1932. Chester County Historical Society, West Chester, PA.

18. Anderson, *Bayard Rustin*, p. 33.

19. Anderson, *Bayard Rustin*, p. 35.

20. *Time on Two Crosses: The Collected Writings of Bayard Rustin,* ed. Devon W. Carbado and Donald Weise (San Francisco: Cleis Press, 2003), p. 283.

21. Anderson, *Bayard Rustin*, p. 37.

22. Anderson, *Bayard Rustin*, p. 45.

23. Haskins, *Bayard Rustin*, p. 19.

24. Anderson, *Bayard Rustin*, p. 56.

25. President Franklin D. Roosevelt, Executive Order 8802, June 25, 1941. See online at **http://eeoc.gov/eeoc/history/35th/thelaw/eo-8802.html**

26. D'Emilio, *Lost Prophet* , p. 46.

27. *Black Fire: African American Quakers on Spirituality and Human Rights.* ed. Harold D. Weaver, Jr., Paul Kriese, and Stephen W. Angell with Anne Steere Nash (Philadelphia: Quaker Press of Friends General Conference, 2011), p. 156.

28. *Time on Two Crosses*, pp. 4–5.

29. *I Must Resist: Bayard Rustin's Life in Letters,* ed. Michael G. Long (San Francisco: City Lights Books, 2012), p. 7.

30. Anderson, *Bayard Rustin*, p. 90.

31. James Haskins, *Bayard Rustin: Behind the Scenes of the Civil Rights Movement* (New York: Hyperion, 1997), p. 30.

32. D'Emilio, *Lost Prophet*, p. 69.

33. Bayard Rustin, *Interracial Primer: How You Can Help Relieve Tension Between Negroes and Whites* (New York: Fellowship of Reconciliation, 1941), pp. 6–14.

34. *I Must Resist*, p. 7.

35. *I Must Resist*, pp. 11–12.

36. D'Emilio, *Lost Prophet*, p. 77.

37. *I Must Resist*, p. 16.

38. *I Must Resist*, pp. 23–24.

39. *I Must Resist*, p. 28.

40. *I Must Resist*, p. 81.

41. *I Must Resist*, p. 70.

42. *I Must Resist*, p. 83.

43. *I Must Resist*, p. 1.

44. Philadelphia Yearly Meeting of the Religious Society of Friends, *Faith and Practice: A Book of Christian Discipline* (adopted 1998). See the online section titled "Extracts from the Writings of Friends > Concerns, Leadings, Testimonies" **http://www.pym.org/faith-and-practice/extracts-from-the-writings-of-friends/concerns-leadings-testimonies/**

45. D'Emilio, *Lost Prophet*, p. 126.

46. *I Must Resist*, p. 95.

47. *I Must Resist*, p. 96.

48. *Time on Two Crosses*, p. 18.

49. Richard Goldstein, "Irene Morgan Kirkaldy, 90, Rights Pioneer, Dies," *New York Times*, August 13, 2007. See at **http://www.nytimes.com/2007/08/13/us/13kirkaldy.html?_r=0**

50. *I Must Resist*, p. 92.

51. *I Must Resist*, p. 110.

52. D'Emilio, *Lost Prophet*, p. 152.

53. *I Must Resist*, p. 115.

54. President Harry S. Truman, Executive Order 9981, July 26, 1948. See online at **http://trumanlibrary.org/9981a.htm**

55. Daniel Levine, *Bayard Rustin and the Civil Rights Movement* (New Brunswick, NJ: Rutgers University Press, 2000), p. 62.

56. *I Must Resist*, p. 123.

57. *Time on Two Crosses*, p. 35.

58. *Time on Two Crosses*, p. 53.

59. *Time on Two Crosses*, p. 32.

60. *I Must Resist*, p. 128.

61. D'Emilio, *Lost Prophet*, p. 190.

62. *I Must Resist*, p. 149.

63. *I Must Resist*, p. 151.

64. D'Emilio, *Lost Prophet*, p. 199.

65. *I Must Resist*, p. 161.

66. David K. Johnson, *The Lavender Scare: The Cold War Persecution of Gays and Lesbians in the Federal Government* (Chicago: University of Chicago Press, 2004), p. 123.

67. *Speak Truth to Power: A Quaker Search for an Alternative to Violence—A Study of International Conflict Prepared for the American Friends Service Committee* (Philadelphia: American Friends Service Committee, 1955), p. 9. See online at **http://www.afsc.org/sites/afsc.civicactions.net/files/documents/Speak_Truth_to_Power.pdf**

68. *Speak Truth to Power*, p. 35.

69. D'Emilio, *Lost Prophet*, p. 228.

70. D'Emilio, *Lost Prophet*, p. 228.

71. D'Emilio, *Lost Prophet*, p. 229.

72. Anderson, *Bayard Rustin*, p. 188.

73. *I Must Resist*, pp. 169–170.

74. Martin Luther King, Jr., *Stride Toward Freedom: The Montgomery Story* (New York: Harper & Row, 1958), pp. 90–92.

75. *I Must Resist*, p. 184.

76. D'Emilio, *Lost Prophet*, p. 337.

77. Martin Luther King, Jr., "Give Us the Ballot," May 17, 1957, Washington, DC. See online at **http://mlk-kpp01.stanford.edu/index.php/kingpapers/article/give_us_the_ballot_address_at_the_prayer_pilgrimage_for_freedom/**

78. *I Must Resist*, p. 212.

79. *I Must Resist*, p. 212.

80. Barry Miles, *Peace: 50 Years of Protest* (Pleasantville, NY: Readers Digest, 2008), pp. 91–92.

81. *I Must Resist*, p. 235.

82. *I Must Resist*, p. 236.

83. *I Must Resist*, p. 237; D'Emilio, *Lost Prophet*, p. 298.

84. *I Must Resist*, p. 257.

85. *I Must Resist*, p. 260.

86. Bayard Rustin, *Strategies for Freedom* (New York: Columbia University Press, 1976), pp. 44–45.

87. *I Must Resist*, p. 260.

88. *I Must Resist*, p. 262.

89. D'Emilio, *Lost Prophet*, p. 347.

90. Susanna McBee, "Organizer of D.C. March Is Dedicated to Nonviolence," *Washington Post*, August 11, 1963.

91. D'Emilio, *Lost Prophet*, p. 348.

92. *I Must Resist*, p. 268.

93. *Time on Two Crosses*, p. 286.

94. *I Must Resist*, p. 269.

95. Anderson, *Bayard Rustin*, p. 255.

96. Words by Langston Hughes, music by Emerson Harper, "I'm Marching Down Freedom Road," 1942. Recording. See online article titled "That's Why We're Marching: WWII and the American Folk Song Movement," Smithsonian/Folkways, 1996, at **http://www.folkways.si.edu/thats-why-were-marching-world-war-ii-and-the-american-folksong-movement/folk-historical-song-struggle-protest/music/album/Smithsonian**

97. Martin Luther King, Jr., "I Have A Dream," August 28, 1963, Washington, D.C. See online at **http://news.bbc.co.uk/2/hi/americas/3170387.stm**

98. "Bayard Rustin Reads the Demands of the March," WGBH Media Library and Archives, Boston, MA. See online at **http://openvault.wgbh.org/catalog/march-777724-bayard-rustin-reads-the-demands-of-the-march**

99. Anderson, *Bayard Rustin*, p. 263.

100. *I Must Resist*, p. 275.

101. Martin Luther King, Jr., "Our God Is Marching On," March 25, 1965, Montgomery, Alabama. See online at **http://mlk-kpp01.stanford.edu/index.php/kingpapers/article/our_god_is_marching_on/**

102. D'Emilio, *Lost Prophet*, p. 421.

103. "August 6, 1965: Voting Rights Act." See online at **http://www.usm.edu/crdp/html/cd/vra65.htm**

104. *I Must Resist*, p. 305.

105. *I Must Resist*, p. 316.

106. *Time on Two Crosses*, p. 116.

107. Anderson, *Bayard Rustin*, p. 305.

108. *I Must Resist*, pp. 345–346.

109. *I Must Resist*, p. 361.

110. *I Must Resist*, p. 361.

111. D'Emilio, *Lost Prophet*, p. 477.

112. *I Must Resist*, p. 416.

113. *I Must Resist*, p. 460.

114. *Time on Two Crosses*, p. 275.

115. *I Must Resist*, p. 462.

116. *Time on Two Crosses*, p. 279.

117. *I Must Resist*, p. 477.

118. Rachel Moston, "Bayard Rustin on His Own Terms," *The Haverford Journal* (February 2005): p. 82. Access PDF of article at **http://thesis.haverford.edu/dspace/handle/10066/959**

119. Benjamin Y. Lowe, "West Chester School to Bear Rustin's Name," *Philadelphia Inquirer*, December 17, 2002. See online at **http://articles.philly.com/2002-12-17/news/25359610_1_board-members-school-board-civil-rights**

120. "50th Anniversary of March on Washington," August 28, 2013, C-Span video, National Cable Satellite Corporation, Washington, D.C. See online at **http://www.c-span.org/video/?c4463194/rev-kristin-stoneking-50th-anniversary-march-washington**

121. "50th Anniversary of March on Washington," August 28, 2013. For Congressman Lewis's remarks, see 3:13:17. See online at **http://www.c-span.org/video/?314757-1/50th-anniversary-march-washington**

122. "50th Anniversary of March on Washington," August 28, 2013. For President Carter's remarks, see 3:19:45. See at **http://www.c-span.org/video/?314757-1/50th-anniversary-march-washington&start=11780**

123. "50th Anniversary of March on Washington," August 28, 2013. For President Clinton's remarks, see 3:30:46. See at **http://www.c-span.org/video/?c4463122/march-washington-anniversary-presidential-portion**

124. "50th Anniversary of March on Washington," August 28, 2013. For President Obama's remarks, see 4:01:36. See at **http://www.c-span.org/video/?c4506443/president-obama-marks-50th-anniversary-march-washington**

125. President Barack Obama, Remarks by the President at the Presidential Medal of Freedom Ceremony, November 20, 2013. See at **http://whitehouse.gov/the-press-office/2013/11/20/remarks-president-presidential-medal-freedom-ceremony**

126. D'Emilio, *Lost Prophet*, p. 16.

BIBLIOGRAPHY

Books

Anderson, Jervis. *Bayard Rustin: Troubles I've Seen*. New York: HarperCollins, 1997.

D'Emilio, John. *Lost Prophet: The Life and Times of Bayard Rustin*. New York: Free Press, 2003.

Haskins, James. *Bayard Rustin: Behind the Scenes of the Civil Rights Movement*. New York: Hyperion, 1997.

I Must Resist: Bayard Rustin's Life in Letters, ed. Michael G. Long. San Francisco: City Lights Books, 2012.

Levine, Daniel. *Bayard Rustin and the Civil Rights Movement*. New Brunswick, NJ: Rutgers University Press, 2000.

Rustin, Bayard. *Interracial Primer: How You Can Help Relieve Tension Between Negroes and Whites*. New York: Fellowship of Reconciliation, 1941. See online at **http://documents.law.yale.edu/bayard-rustin-centennial/ interracial-primer-0**.

————. *Strategies for Freedom*. New York: Columbia University Press, 1976.

Time on Two Crosses: The Collected Writings of Bayard Rustin, ed. Devon W. Carbado and Donald Weise. San Francisco: Cleis Press, 2003.

Others

Bayard Rustin Papers, 1942–1987. Library of Congress, Washington, D.C.
    Correspondence, speeches, notes, reports, press releases, financial records, and other papers documenting Bayard's "leading role as an activist in the African American civil rights movement, advocate of international human rights and social reform, and pacifist." See collection summary at **http://hdl.loc.gov/loc.mss/eadmss.ms996004**.

FBI Records of Bayard Rustin. Federal Bureau of Investigation, Washington, D.C.
    Reports on the FBI's surveillance of Bayard; the FBI considered Bayard a threat to national security. See some of the files online at **http://vault.fbi.gov/bayard-rustin**.

Nancy Kates, Bennett L. Singer, Mridu Chandra, Erik Todd Dellums, Bobby Shepard, and B. Quincy Griffin. *Brother Outsider: The Life of Bayard Rustin*. San Francisco: California Newsreel, 2002.

> One and one-half hour DVD of a program that was broadcast on public TV. It shows the life of Bayard Rustin with interviews from people who knew him well. See more information at
> **http://www.pbs.org/pov/brotheroutsider/**.

"Pacifism and the American Civil Rights Movement: A Celebration of the Centennial of Bayard Rustin (1912–2012)." 2012. The Yale Law School Library Document Collection Center, Lillian Goldman Library, Yale University, New Haven, CT.

> This online exhibit shows important documents and photographs related to Bayard's work as a pacifist leader in the United States. See the exhibit at **http://documents.law.yale.edu/bayard-rustin**.

"The Reminiscences of Bayard Rustin." Fourteen interviews with Bayard Rustin, November 14, 1984 through June 18, 1987. Columbia University Oral History Project, Columbia University, New York, NY.

> These personal memories shared by Bayard are not yet available online.

ABOUT THE AUTHORS

Jacqueline Houtman is a freelance writer. She holds a Ph.D. in Medical Microbiology and Immunology from The University of Wisconsin—Madison. Her science writing for adults and children has appeared in *World Book Science Year*, Federation of American Societies for Experimental Biology's *Breakthroughs in Bioscience* series, *Cleveland Clinic Magazine*, The Dana Foundation's *Progress in Brain Research, The Dana Sourcebook of Immunology* and numerous academic and educational publications. Her award-winning novel for young readers, *The Reinvention of Edison Thomas* (Boyds Mills Press), was chosen for five state reading lists. Houtman and her husband obtained their Quaker marriage license in Bayard's home-town of West Chester, Pennsylvania. They live in Madison, Wisconsin, where she is a member of Madison Monthly Meeting.

Walter Naegle was Bayard Rustin's partner for a decade. The two met in 1977, when Bayard was dividing his time between domestic civil rights issues and international affairs—especially refugee work and human rights advocacy. Walter had long been interested in nonviolence and social justice issues, and he and Bayard shared values, interests, and beliefs. After graduating from Fordham University, he began working with Bayard at the A. Philip Randolph Educational Fund. When Bayard died in 1987, Walter was instrumental in establishing The Bayard Rustin Fund, a private foundation that promotes Bayard's values and works to heighten awareness of his accomplishments. In 2013 he accepted a posthumous Presidential Medal of Freedom for Bayard at the White House, one of the first same-sex partners to do so.

Michael G. Long is an associate professor of religious studies and peace and conflict studies at Elizabethtown College and is the author or editor of several books on civil rights, religion and politics, and peacemaking in mid-century America, including *Gay Is Good: The Life and Letters of Gay Rights Pioneer Franklin Kameny* (Syracuse University Press); *Beyond Home Plate: Jackie Robinson on Life after Baseball* (Syracuse University Press); *Martin Luther King, Jr., Homosexuality, and the Early Gay Rights Movement* (Palgrave Macmillan); *I Must Resist: Bayard Rustin's Life in Letters* (City Lights); *Marshalling Justice: The Early Civil Rights Letters of Thurgood*

Marshall (Amistad/HarperCollins); and *First Class Citizenship: The Civil Rights Letters of Jackie Robinson* (Times Books). Another of Long's books, *Christian Peace and Nonviolence*, focuses on international peacemaking efforts by Christian activists and scholars. Long's work has been featured or reviewed in *The New York Times, The Washington Post, The Los Angeles Times, The Boston Globe, USA Today*, CNN, *Book Forum, Ebony/Jet*, and many other newspapers and journals. Long blogs for the Huffington Post and has appeared on C-Span and NPR. His speaking engagements have taken him from the National Archives in Washington, DC, to the Schomberg Center of the New York Public Library in Harlem, and to the City Club of San Diego. Long holds a Ph.D. from Emory University in Atlanta and resides in Highland Park, Pennsylvania.

INDEX

ACKNOWLEDGMENTS

The authors are deeply grateful to the following individuals and institutions: the Estate of Bayard Rustin; Publications and Distribution Committee at QuakerPress of Friends General Conference (FGC); Jonathan Vogel-Borne, publisher of QuakerPress of FGC; Chel Avery, formerly of QuakerPress of FGC; The Sara Bowers Fund of Kennett (PA) Friends Meeting; Becky Birtha; the staff at the Manuscripts Division of the Library of Congress (which houses the Bayard Rustin Papers); the staff at the Prints and Photographs Division of the Library of Congress; Wendy Chmielewski, curator of the Swarthmore College Peace Collection; Margaret Chisholm of Yale Law School Library; Rachelle Horowitz; Sylvia Morra and Louise Hyder-Darlington of High Library at Elizabethtown College; Rob Lukens and Pamela Powell of the Chester County Historical Society; John D'Emilio; Mandy Carter; Bennett Singer; Nancy Kates; Jervis Anderson; Daniel Levine; James Haskins; Karin, Jack, and Nate Long; Sharon Herr; Elaine Benedetti; Dean Fletcher McClellan of Elizabethtown College; Sallie Jones; Madison (WI) Monthly Meeting; the Wisconsin Chapter of the Society of Children's Book Writers and Illustrators; the Cooperative Children's Book Center; Carl, Ethan, and Melinda Houtman; the dedicated crew at City Lights Books, and especially Chantz Erolin, who was a sheer gift to us as we wrapped up countless details near the end of production; Emma Hager and Jessica Cox for their work on the index; and Bayard Taylor Rustin.